THE CHRIST SPIRIT

D1358153

DALE LANDRY
EDITED BY: RICHARD GLAESSER

Assistant Editors: Richard LeBlanc & Christine Zeldin
Cover Illustration & Design: Jock MacRae
Photo Imaging: Jurek Wyszynski

3rd
EYE
PUBLISHING

Copyright Page

© 1999 by Dale Landry

3rd Eye Publishing
c/o Hushion House Publishing Limited
36 Northline Road
Toronto, Ontario
Canada M4B 3E2

The Access Publishers Network Inc.
6893 Sullivan Rd.
Brawn, Michigan
U.S.A. 49637

The Christ Spirit
ISBN 0-9684678-1-4

Dale Landry

Editor: Richard Glaesser
Assistant Editors: Richard LeBlanc & Christine Zeldin
Cover Illustration & Design: Jock MacRae
Photo Imaging: Jurek Wyszynski

Quantity discounted orders are available for groups. Please make enquiries by writing directly to the publisher.

Printing history
Printed in Canada

DEDICATION

This book is dedicated to my sister, Sarah, who has stood strong beside me and risked it all.

To a wonderful friend and companion Rick who has made each of these books a reality with persistence, dedication, love, a lot of hard work and very long days and late nights. My gratitude goes beyond words and feelings for making dreams for me come true.

To Catharine who has been a wonderful support and friend for the past eleven years. Her thoughts and words have inspired me, calmed the rough waters and created a continual atmosphere of love. Thank you Catharine.

To the 'Three Musketeers,' David, Natalie and Charles, for all of their kindness and generosity.

And lastly but certainly not least, I dedicate "The Christ Spirit" to each individual who has helped me by working with me and developing through my classes and supporting me in all of my endeavours.

ABOUT THE AUTHOR

Since 1983, Dale Landry has developed his visionary gift as a trance channeller. Graduating with a Bachelor of Arts in Psychology, Dale works with many individuals helping them in their spiritual quest for personal growth and development.

FOREWORD

The art of channelling is about reaching into your subconscious mind and retrieving information. The knowledge you can gain through this experience is available to anyone if he or she desires it. For example, if you wish to know your purpose and you ask over and over in your thoughts to receive this information your subconscious will pick up the message after a short period of time and deliver the information you desire.

Each person is capable of achieving his or her goals with the possible exception of those who are limited by a developmental disability. However, these people who are mentally challenged have a number of gifts that the average person may not even realize, namely, unconditional love.

The practice of channelling involves lowering your body's energy and setting your conscious mind aside in order to allow a soul from spirit to enter your body and deliver information. This skill takes years of work although most individuals have the ability to do it.

Allowing the essence of Christ's spirit to come forward and speak through me to provide information has been at a minimum an insightful experience I am not capable of putting into words. Throughout each session of "The Christ Spirit", I felt Jesus Christ in the way he is generally believed to be: loving, kind and compassionate, and I learned that I also had the ability to understand and love myself and everyone around me.

Channelling Jesus Christ provided me the opportunity to unlock the many doors to my soul and to reach forth and obtain a higher understanding of my spirit.

For many, each new day is a seemingly different struggle, but to move beyond your problems and find your heart within you must start on a new path of inner peace and contentment. "The Christ Spirit" was not written to prove the existence of Christ some 2,000 years ago but instead to show that Christ is still with us today in the hearts of each and every person.

Dale Landry

PROLOGUE*

THE LANGUAGE OF LOVE

When I lived, there was a story I often told to those who gathered to listen. It was about a young boy named David who spent most of his time playing alone but at times he worked closely with his father. One day David's father passed away, and because he did not understand death he was confused and pained, and no longer wanted to play or do the things he used to. As this young boy grew older, he approached life with a serious attitude. There was little laughter and no desire for love because inwardly he felt that he had also died with his father. David had no explanation for his feelings and did not feel the same desires as other young people his age. But one day, David met a new friend, another young man, and they immediately became kindred spirits. They came together often, never tiring of one another's company. Soon David realized that once again his heart felt light and there was love for his companion.

Initially, the thought of loving someone so strongly frightened him, however the idea of letting him go was also too much to bear. So together as friends they grew into manhood and David's friend soon found a wife and settled down. While the nature of their friendship had changed due to the marriage, there was still a strong connection of love. However, instead of marrying, David decided to travel to foreign lands which to him was a marriage of sorts, a life journey unlike what others would commit to. He travelled for many years and met many strange and wonderful people. David found the experience often difficult and lonely but at other times experienced great compassion and love.

Years later, David decided to return home and upon his arrival his old friend was there to greet him. They embraced and spoke as if they had never parted. His friend asked about his travels and David explained all that he had seen and the riches of his experience. In return, David asked his friend about his journey. "I have seen much," said David's

*The prologue for "The Christ Spirit" was delivered by Jesus Christ through Dale Landry during the final session of this book.

friend, "because in all the places you have travelled, all the people you have met, all the love that you have felt, you shared these things with me in my heart and now I am rewarded from your experience."

David remained quiet listening to his friend and then said, "My reward was knowing that you were always there with me and your communication of love kept me safe. And now that I have returned home, I am aware of your experience of love."

The following day, David passed away; the only people who came to his burial were his friend and his son. The son asked his father, "Who was this man? Was he your friend?" The father replied, "He was to me what the moon is to the stars, what the wind is to the earth, and what the water is to a sailboat." "What do you mean?" the son asked. The father looked at his son as the tears rolled from his eyes and said, "I could never tell you how much you mean to me. My love for you is so strong that it is difficult for me to put into words the breath of life that this friend has given to me. But whether he is here with me or not, like yourself, he will always be the wind in my sails that carries me through the troubled waters into the night's setting sun."

SESSION 1

It is difficult to explain my past, the present, and what will come about in the future. There are many thoughts and doubts about myself, God, Heaven, Hell and what lies in between.

Generally, it is believed that my purpose for existing in your world was to show people the way towards peace, kindness, understanding and compassion. But this was only a small part of my overall purpose. In my true purpose, I desired a completion and a need to pass through many physical expressions[1] to understand God and spirit.

It is believed that God chose me to show others the path to freedom, the key to heaven's gate, and the ability to move beyond your physical reality and recognize that there is a world hereafter.

Looking back on my life as Jesus Christ, I believe I failed at being someone I thought I was supposed to be. It was never recognized or even understood that I was just like everybody else – human first and Godly second, although both are one and the same. To live in this physical world, you are one part God and one part human, two sides to the same coin that move in seemingly different directions.

People believe that I knew everything and therefore never doubted my path. But there were many times I had doubts, and many times I believed I was alone in a world that seemed harsh and unforgiving.

The miracles I performed were true miracles. However, you can perform a miracle if you simply open up your heart to the creative force known to you as God. It has become difficult to achieve this feat because the information on how to open your heart and to change your energy in this physical world has been lost.

I did not desire death on the cross, yet I was aware of my fate even from a youthful age. Like many others, however, I denied my fateful end.

---

1 Physical expression denotes the idea of a physical life. It is said that the soul of each living person exists in many different lifetimes: past, present and future—and this is referred to as a physical expression.

Throughout history, people have prayed to me and asked for guidance but not once has anyone asked to live the life I lived. The power within my soul when I lived in your physical world is something that men and women have tried to emulate but no one has achieved the same capabilities with the same level of responsibility or desire for compassion, kindness and love. Perhaps it is due to my fate and the fear of punishment at the hands of their peers for why no one has asked to be like me. I did not realize the kind of punishment I was to endure at my life's end.

If you wish to praise and love me, and if you desire me to reside alongside you with all of my good purposes, then you must do the same in turn. To do so, however, is difficult because you fear the responsibility of being so Godly. Your attachment to your physical life keeps you in denial and pain rather than offering you hope, love and light. You believe that the world in which you live is dark but the darkness is only the fear you hold within your soul and your heart. You are frightened to break free of this darkness and therefore you perpetuate the pain and ignorance that comes with living in your physical world.

I have not reincarnated as Christ but I have taken on many other physical vibrations[2] of a much lesser purpose. Each individual has a purpose that is part of the collective purpose and every living soul works together to progress forward in your physical reality. Your world is a one-dimensional vibration, a one-way mirror. From spirit, we can see you but you cannot see us. We know you are there and you may believe we exist. However, you fear the spirit world because you are not completely certain that we truly exist beyond the veil[3].

I do not wish to speak to you now about the rights or wrongs of your world, nor am I here to open a door to let each of you pass through. I am here because I have been called upon to speak. This does not mean that I will appear each time I am summoned, but if I am asked, I will provide you the answers you desire. I may not speak to you, however, in the way you expect or would want me to.

2 Like a physical expression, a physical vibration has its own physical reality. In order to inhabit the earth, a soul from spirit must lower is vibration or its energy, to a point where it can physically inhabit the earth.

3 In this case, the veil can be understood as the shield dividing the physical and metaphysical world. The metaphysical world encompasses all souls in spirit; the place where each living soul will return once they have died.

Through prayer, you may consider it a fortunate circumstance to have me as a guest at your dinner table and you do have that opportunity. But, when I am called upon in prayer or meditation, I am perceived as a higher being who knows more than you, and if I am viewed as a soul of higher knowledge, I am kept at a distance because I am considered out of reach. So, if I am at a distance, I cannot truly share my thoughts, feelings and spirit with you. Call upon me as your equal to bless the food you are about to receive, to join you in your home and share in your energy, love, compassion and insight. Then, together as one, we will have purpose, and I can willingly share my knowledge and love as a friend. I cannot offer you the love you deserve if I am a stranger at a distance.

Ask yourself what I truly mean to you. Do you understand why I was created in the eyes of God? Although I am considered to be a savior, how can I save you if you are not willing to save yourself? If I show you the way to truth, light and the answers needed to gain inner peace, will you use this information or will you expect me to enter your home and do the work for you? Will I be required to feel your pain because you are unable to feel it or can you see that you are capable of feeling the pain as well?

God has many expressions and you are a part of them. To know God is to know yourself, for God is a mirror of what lies within as well as outside of yourself. Your hopes and beliefs of being set free to be with God is each person's desire for inner contentment and peace.

You believe you have lost sight of your true goals for existence but you have not. It is simply hidden from view to help you in your inner growth and development.

Why is there so much sickness and pain and so little love, compassion and kindness in the world? The answer is within yourself, not with society. As you change and give more love, kindness and peace of mind to yourself, your world will be that much closer to feeling complete and whole in its purpose. You must come to a point where you can accept your fellow peers and live together in harmony. This goal may appear impossible or overwhelming at the outset but with inner work, you can understand your purpose for existing in this physical world.

You do not have to accept my words as truth or fact. Simply read the information with an open mind and heart. Do not judge harshly what you may think is wrong or right. Think only in your thoughts that you are allowed to see me in many different ways and from many different perspectives. The beauty of life is not always knowing whether something is true or false but that it merely exists as you exist in a reality that is not always understood or recognized.

As the soul Jesus Christ, I have many desires. They are not as you might imagine them to be. I do not desire physical wealth, love between two souls or the release of pain and sickness. My desires are simple. I wish that soon you will be able to see your world through my eyes and understand that there is no need to maintain your materialistic dreams. This is what I believe to be freedom.

I reach out to you and know from my vision of what the future will bring that you too are reaching back.

SESSION 2

The doorway to knowledge is difficult to unlock because most people try to avoid the work required to discover new information. Knowledge brings change and with change comes healing, insight and forgiveness. To forgive is the ultimate achievement in the Divine plan; it will allow you to understand and learn more about love. Love has many different vibrations and the more you can forgive, the more your love will expand and grow. Love can conquer all but it cannot heal without forgiveness even though healing is at the root of love. My thoughts are simple: to heal you must forgive and through forgiveness you can express love.

As a child, I quickly learned the ways of my elders. Through example, they taught me how to assist myself and others. I was a very quick learner and constantly absorbed information about life's treasures and secrets. At night when I went to bed, angels would appear and talk to me about my purpose, my growth, the people around me and how I could learn more. I would tell others about my conversations with the angels and they would look at me in amazement, not because I spoke with angels, but because of what the angels told me. When I was young, I believed that all children spoke to angels and not for a moment did I ever consider myself exceptional. At the age of nine, I realized that the adults who I saw as possessing great wisdom did not have the same opportunity as me to speak with the angels. In one sense it was disheartening because I felt alone in a world I did not understand and if others did not speak to angels, how was it possible that angels truly existed? But, they felt as real to me as my family.

When I spoke with angels, they talked to me about my hands and their healing abilities. They explained that in time I could heal anyone I touched: this was my gift from God and I was the only individual alive who had this ability. I believed everything the angels said since I had no reason to doubt them.

I was amazed by the angels' beauty. They possessed great knowledge and wisdom, and when they spoke, it was like listening to a chorus of wonderful singers. Sometimes we would have conversations late into the night yet rarely was I tired when I awoke in the morning.

There is much about my past that is still unknown, thus, to talk about my youth will give people a greater sense of how I came to understand my purpose. You too can speak with the angels. They may not appear before your eyes but they do surround you nevertheless.

When I was a child, I questioned if I would marry and have children. To this query, the angels explained that I could obtain whatever I desired. What I did not realize at the time was that I had already chosen my path.

With maturity and age, I grew wiser and quickly learned that few individuals were capable of teaching me because I became more of a teacher to them. This was a great disappointment to me as I wondered why I was living in a world filled with so many adults and children who knew so little of their own purpose and of God? God and life purpose appeared unimportant to others but they were all consuming to me. I needed to know the secrets of why we existed, and why there was pain, struggle, denial and hardship. It was difficult to obtain information about these important things because no matter where I turned, it appeared people knew little about the God they seemingly loved so much. It was a challenge to understand everything I did at a youthful age as I could not verify its validity. Instinctively, however, I knew the information I received was truth and that everything else around me appeared to be an illusion. I was obviously confused by this paradox.

In my youth I sought solace in the desert because it was the only place where I could find refuge from my difficulties. However, once there, I soon realized that I was unable to run away for too long. Visions of my future would begin to appear. I had images of people dying in wars long after my death and the more I saw the heavier my heart felt. I had yet to understand my life purpose or the reason for these visions but I would watch in amazement as one vision after another would appear.

It may sound strange but from the time I was three, I often had visions of a man hanging from a cross. I could not foretell who that man was until the day of my death, and it was only in that moment, on that day, that I fully understood the reason and purpose of my life. When I died, I reflected on my life as a dream, one that had many beautiful moments but was also painful from beginning to end. It would be simplistic to say that I saved so many souls when truly there were only a few.

I could not accept that the people I loved and cherished could turn against me so strongly when I meant them no harm or ill. My disciples also turned against me in the end and only one truly loved me without fear. To all of them, I was an enigma; I was relegated to the status of a great leader but not a fighter as they had expected. John the Baptist knew me and understood my fate but he was not prepared for what was to be the end of his life.

Looking back at my existence, I realize I never experienced a true friendship since everyone I met expected something from me. I gave freely of myself, for I was told by the angels that it was my purpose to do so, and through this good will my cup would always be full. Therefore, I gave as much as I could. My cross to bear was not in dying but in living a hollow existence without anyone who recognized or understood my purpose.

People who came to listen, enjoyed hearing me speak as if I was a singing angel. However, no one understood the essence of my words. Although I always had a captive audience, I felt they could not hear. Ultimately, my message reached no one. Even now, the words that are considered my own are still repeated, debated, argued over and criticized by the masses. Unfortunately, the main idea of my message is still not recognized.

It was only at the time of my death that I finally understood the words which I had spoken throughout my life. This catharsis came to me as a great wave of understanding. I can best describe my comprehension in one simple word—forgiveness. Forgive the people for they know not what they do, and forgive myself for I had no understanding of why I believed I needed to do what I did. To give of myself was a part of me; it came from inside and I had to fulfill this purpose. Those I spoke to, however, did not understand the words I had spoken. So now I ask, is it really God who does not want you to hear? Ask God why you cannot hear and look to see what is presented to you. Even if you pray to me, Jesus Christ, and ask to see the light, I cannot show you the things you refuse to see and hear. You are the only one who can turn the key to your own heart, to the place called home, the home where your heart resides. To go inside of your home is to make a personal discovery. In your physical world, it is impossible to truly hear with your physical ears or to fully see with your physical eyes. It is only through your heart that you can look inwardly and understand your reason for existing. I was not meant to know my purpose until death, but inwardly I discovered most, if not all, the secrets to life and living.

I loved children because they accepted me as a human being without judgement or the need to be led. They simply wanted to be with me and understand me in the moment we were together. It is only in youth that a child can use his or her physical capabilities, to understand the moment and the freedom it can bring. However, as the child grows older, physical sight and physical hearing begin to wane.

SESSION 3

When I lived, there was a common belief that people became sick because they did something wrong or evil. Sickness was disguised and hidden by family and friends and it was believed that if a family member was ill the family was being punished or shamed. These beliefs have been perpetuated over time and still today sickness is considered a punishment and disgrace before peers, family and society. Even though sickness is a common occurrence, people who become ill believe that they have done something wrong. Most understand the fallacy of this idea but this perception still exists; many believe that perhaps the ill person has either done too much, worked too hard, not worked hard enough or kept the wrong company. Common sense tells us that sickness and disease are common occurrences and that everyone will encounter some form of illness in his or her life.

Death is also looked upon as shameful. Whether it results from cancer, heart failure, disease or an accident, there is a subtle belief that if the person who died had done something more noble or had been more aware, he or she would not have passed over so needlessly.

Through my healing abilities, the multitudes learned to believe that God could work miracles and that the common person was not lost. When I existed, only the wealthiest were not rejected and were even respected for their illnesses. The rich were allowed to be sick because they had power and financial worth. Death for them was viewed as a transformational stage where God helped to cleanse them and rid them of all evil spirits and deeds. The poor and unfortunate, however, were viewed as evil, undesirable and diseased. I became a champion for the masses because I showed people how to rise above their infirmities. The poor craved someone or something to believe in, whereas the rich and the strong feared the poor possessing the same knowledge and strength.

You are taught to believe that only God can rid you of your afflictions. But what I believed and taught is that God resides in each person and it is up to the God within you to heal and release yourself from the pains that you hold. You cannot blame society for any wrong because you are a part of society. To change the world you must first change from within. To break the ties that bind your hands and feet, you do not need to destroy your captor but to understand why you have been captured. When you can come to understand your captor and why you are imprisoned, you will understand yourself, your blindness, your anger and your shame. As you begin to love your captor, you will learn to love the parts of yourself that you dislike.

People want to know if I will return for a second or possibly even a third coming. Some still wait for my arrival as they were not present at my crucifixion; they pray for my return to see me die needlessly as a means of absolving them from their sins.

When I come again, I will not appear as the Jesus Christ I was. I know that history repeats itself, and in this regard, I do not have the desire to be a historical sacrifice for the masses, a religion or a faith. I am within each of you, disguised as it may be, cloaked in a different way than you may expect. It is easy to touch you from this side of the veil but most if not all would question if this connection is possible. When I was crucified, people also wondered whether I had in fact touched them or they had just imagined me.

I now reside within each of you, disguised as it may be, in a different way than you might expect. To embrace me is to embrace a part of yourself known as God or what you believe to be God. But embracing God will not remove you from your pain or confusion; it will likely increase it. Embracing God will only cause you to ask more questions, desire more answers and work harder at understanding life. To have more questions means acquiring more ideas and a more rewarding pathway, yet this will itself present more difficulties.

It is now common in your time to easily access all of the things you desire; to quickly travel, to effortlessly obtain work and to be given leisure time. But in this time of leisure and the ease in which you can easily obtain all the things you want, are you provided more fulfillment or pain because with greater leisure there is too much time to fill?

You may wonder why God or spirit does not unveil itself to the masses. You may ask why we do not give you signs of our existence and help you to progress forward? This is the great mystery and those who doubt the existence of God or spirit are the very people who question their own existence. If God or myself had to prove our existence, your inner work would cease and there would be no purpose for inhabiting the earth. You need to prove it to yourself. To understand the purpose of your existence, you must first determine for yourself the reason why you want to know this information. To simply remain in your pain and to believe that you are misfortunate is an excuse to avoid undertaking the inner work required. If you were a student and decided to stop your studies, no one would be harmed but yourself for you would be less knowledgeable about your own world. It is crucial to your own personal development that you not see others as wiser or more fortunate, but as holding different talents than yourself. People who are physically blind and deaf can still learn to see and hear, if they rely on their other senses to understand their world, just as those who are mentally or physically challenged, can use their heart to feel and see their surroundings.

The day before my death, The Archangel Michael came to sit with me. I was alone in a garden pondering my direction when he appeared; he was incredibly radiant, more so than the other times when he had come to me. At first I did not understand why he had appeared, but when he spoke I realized he had come to bring a message he could not easily say. He said to me that the next day my heart would betray me but that I did not need to fear it. In my insight and wisdom, I knew Michael was not telling me the full truth but I did not dare question an angel of God. I now can see that he came as a guide, to let me know that regardless of where I was, he would always be there for me. From the time of my birth to the time of my death, Michael was with me at all times, and true to his word my heart did betray me, but not as I had expected. Through my death, I realized that the physical heart has a longing to exist on earth; it betrayed me in my desire to stay when I knew I had to leave. In your heart lies the doorway between your physical reality and spirit and you must pass through it, as small as the eye of the needle, to reach what you know as Heaven. To pass through the heart from your physical reality into spirit is incredibly painful and your heart will desire the love of your physical world. However, it will learn to love even more the knowledge and wisdom you will gain in spirit.

You thirst for a knowledge and understanding of life's trials and tribulations but do you drink the water when it is placed before you or do you wait until death is close at hand when you will be forced to go out and search for it? My love for the desert was my understanding of the nourishment it had to offer, for as dry and barren as the desert was, my thirst for knowledge, wisdom and understanding was ultimately quenched. There in the desert, in the arid dryness, the hot sun and the burning sands, I understood what hell was all about. However, it was also in the desert that I found an oasis of resources and the love that resided within myself. It was in the hot desert sun that I understood God and what He created. Hell is only an extension of what you see as Heaven, and to live within your physical world is like living in the desert with no water, under a hot sun, with seemingly no God. Living in hell is like having to survive in the desert. If you travel through the desert, you will understand the creatures that survive there and then you can understand yourself. Through that physical hell, you can find the heaven that will take you to a spiritual place on earth. In your reality you have a heaven and a hell and the only thing in between is earth. In your physical world, it is your heart which stands between heaven and hell and serves as a doorway between both worlds. To be lost between Heaven and hell is what the Christians call purgatory. Purgatory is a mirror where one can get lost; in purgatory, you can never travel to Heaven or hell, you can never understand, you can never know, you can never feel nor can you ever express.

You may ask if love truly exists. My question to you is, do you exist? To know and feel love is to first be love. If the ancient scrolls were found and my own writings unearthed, what could I say further that I have not already said? In your soul is a part of me and you will know this if you listen closely to yourself and what I have said. The words I say are locked away tightly within you; you must ask to have them released.

It is not commonly known that before my death, my mother Mary also passed away. She was not there physically at the foot of my cross but appeared in full clothing as I passed into spirit; that is why people believe she was still alive at my crucifixion. These things that I am saying are not from the Bible. There are no history books to verify my facts; you need only ask yourself.

SESSION 4

To realize your true potential is probably one of the most difficult tasks you will have to accomplish, intellectually, creatively and otherwise. There is a constant desire to improve yourself, to learn and understand more, and inevitably to feel complete or more fulfilled.

My purpose as a leader was to show people that they were connected to God and that they had not been abandoned or left alone. Their desire to have purpose and importance was paramount in their lives just as you desire the same things. I ask, do you have an impact on the people around you? Do you believe that after your death you will be remembered or will your memory fade quickly from people's thoughts?

It is correct to assume that everyone has purpose but as the days go by and one year blends into another, it is easy to forget your objective. Many have the tendency to believe that the young are foolish and the old are weak; not a strong combination for a love potion. In my eyes, the old have strength of years and the youth have a desire to learn.

There are two volumes of books that presently exist in your world. The books are each located in Egypt, buried in a tomb, still unearthed. The books were written long before I existed, but during my lifetime as Christ, I had the opportunity to view the both of them. These books are highly regarded as an explanation for why the human race exists. The origin of the books is unknown, but after reading them at the age of nine, I believe that they were created from pure thought at the beginning of time. The books are a guideline to human evolution, the reason for human existence and the eventual fate of humanity. These books have little to do with history but more to do with what I will call 'vision' for these two volumes provide great insight. To read them would require you to understand twelve different languages, plus a thirteenth unspoken language based on hidden sight; it is a language of knowingness and understanding that lies beyond the veil. The other twelve languages, are also not what you would necessarily understand as a language, for they are more reflective of universal laws and each universal law is in itself a language. For example, to love your sister and brother as you would love your parents is a law and a language unto itself just as to respect others as well as yourself may also be considered another language. These books were written to chronicle a story where you and everyone who ever existed and will exist throughout time are living out a portion of this history. In these books I am noted as being a part of God, not as Jesus Christ.

These two books will become unearthed in ten years time. They were discovered in 1909 but were simply passed over by accident, or so it would seem. In the year 2009, they shall resurface once again but within a year or two they will suspiciously disappear. Their appearance will cause quite a stir but may not gain universal notoriety.

If you viewed yourself as a book, you would discover many revealing things upon opening the covers beyond simply a beginning, a middle and an end. You would discover an important story where you are both author and reader who can rewrite your history, recreate your story and come to a final resting place at the end of your journey, one that is both enriching and rewarding.

To further explain these books, it is important to state that the visions I had while reading them appeared as if I were holding the universe in my hands, as the eyes within my soul looked outward to view it all. These two volumes encompassed all that ever existed, and the potential that is described within them is beyond your imagination.

Upon viewing these books, I was in awe of the incredible opportunities that lay unrevealed within what we know as God. To imagine your current knowledge magnified a billion times would give you only a small iota of the information that encompasses this universe and beyond. To learn to unleash your true potential would allow you to change forms, move physical objects, alter your vibration, levitate, heal illness and physically manifest anything that can exist. You would also become capable of hearing and seeking beyond your physical world into other dimensions of thought and spirit. It is for this reason that you are frightened of expressing your true self, and it is also the reason why you have never sought to be like me, in fear of what you are incapable of handling. To unleash the power of your thoughts would be equivalent to a massive explosion in your physical reality that you would find difficult to comprehend.

If you possessed the capabilities and were provided the opportunity to read these two volumes you would discover the reason for human existence. But if provided with this information, would you still have a purpose to live? Of course the answer is yes. As I have already explained, you know the reason why you exist but you fear this knowledge and understanding. To desire more wisdom is not foolishness or ignorance although people who search within are often perceived as such. Those who seek a deeper meaning to life are initially considered a threat by their peers because people fear another's enhanced capability to see and achieve what they desire.

My visions and insight did not please everyone. Even those who believed in me feared my words and capabilities because they did not understand my language of thought. On the one hand, they felt secure emotionally and remained by my side but on the other hand, they looked upon me as irrational and desired that I be challenged and put away so they could be left once again to their own devices and fears. Not once however did I believe I would be challenged since there was no one who possessed more knowledge than I, and that in itself was a great disappointment.

My death was a mistake as anyone who came into contact with me knew well that I was wise and incapable of any wrong doing. The soldiers, clergy and politicians became silent when I was in their presence. I did not need to hush them or ask for their ears. Instinctively their souls quieted and they recognized that they had to listen. I had no fear of death because I did not expect it. However, on my way to the cross, I saw that each soul around me was in a trance-like state, unaware of what was to occur, but continuing methodically to carry out their actions. It was the fear of persecution that caused my own people to deny my existence. They believed I caused harm and hardship, and they did not see me as one who could release them from their persecution, nor do I believe I relieved anyone of their persecution. I did, however, avail myself to the many who sought to have sight.

It is peculiar to communicate in the way that I am speaking now for it seems that while these words will be read, understood and in certain ways heard, the same mistakes will occur until humankind eventually releases itself from the pain and allows itself to become one with fate.

SESSION 5

There are no records of my birth and there remains a lot of confusion about the exact time and date of my death. The reason why the timing of my birth is unknown is because my parents were forced to keep it a secret. I was born virtually two months before the time you now celebrate as my birth date.

In the year I was born, there was a great deal of chaos as it was a well-known prophecy that a saviour or a King was to be born to the Israelites, the so-called "King of the Jews". During that period, however, there were many other predictions about the future but what was unknown was how quickly word of my birth would spread. However, I was not to physically rule in the way my existence was predicted. The Jewish people believed I would lead them out of their pain and hardship while others expected me to be a noble and just King who would help the common people.

Around the time of my birth there were many soothsayers and the gift of second sight was a common phenomena. There was little to foretell about the future but many prophets used the titles of visionaries first and astronomers second. It was obvious that at that time in history people lacked food and poverty was common. Only a few had the means to maintain a good life.

In speaking to those with means my initial role was to show them how to distribute their wealth, to make people happy and to help them improve their commerce. During the time I lived people generally marketed their own goods and sold their wares in the market place. It was common for everyone to have something to sell in the market, including the clergy and the politicians. In assisting those who were wiser and wealthier, I was able to ensure the poor were fed and the sick had their needs attended to.

At the age of five and six, I had the wisdom of a man who was 42 years old and knowledge that far surpassed my age. People agreed to my suggestions because they were in awe of my knowledge and wisdom at such a young age. They believed that for one so young to speak so wisely, the words I spoke must have been true, and they blindly followed my suggestions.

To speak inside the temples and the synagogues was a challenge for anyone, therefore I was never asked to speak at the pulpit. Instead, I would go to a place of worship, seek out the individual who looked like they were in command and ask them a question about God. Their interest would be peaked because they would want to impress upon me their ideas and they would seek to engage me in conversation. Quickly, however, they realized that what I had to say made more sense than what they had been taught and shortly thereafter others would also gather around me to listen. Within a short time, there would be eight to ten clergy gathered around as well as other individuals who were also enthralled by my conversation.

As the word spread that there was a young child who knew so much, the elders of many different faiths and religions became worried. They knew I posed a threat and they feared that before too long the pillars of their religious beliefs would crumble. Therefore, from the early age of four, many religious elders began to plot against me and developed schemes to discredit me. But the more they plotted, the more difficult it became for them because each situation they created turned back on themselves. By the age of ten, there was nowhere I travelled to that people did not know of me. Many wanted to touch my cloak to feel that I was real. They were not in awe of my power or my greatness, they simply had heard rumours of what I knew and spoke of. Because I was so young and spoke so wisely, I was recognized as the leader the prophets had envisioned to be the King of the Jews.

At the age of ten and-a-half, I was asked by my own people, the Jews, to lead them in their faith. They beseeched upon me to show them the way towards God, to leave my beliefs and teachings behind and to follow the ways of my people. I declined. I knew at that time that I did not exist to be a voice for just one group; I was a voice unto myself. Christianity as a basic term simply means the way of the people; those who follow in my footsteps will find their own voice and their own way. However the doctrine, the beliefs and the followings of Christianity have become confused and muddled over time and my

18

voice has been lost to a world consumed with consuming. I spoke to people of all religious faiths, denominations and races. There was no need to hold true to one belief other than the belief in God.

Following the decline of my own people, the Jews, I was turned away. I became an outcast to the very people I had chosen to be born into. It was a lesson I was forced to learn and one that is still being learned today. Those that love you the most always expect the greatest from you and those that love you the least have the fewest expectations. Thus, the poor embraced me as their own, not because I was wise but because they had no one to lead them. No one else took the opportunity to recognize that they were important and that they had souls as well.

For five years after the age of 10, I moved to a land where I could work with spiritual teachers to assist me in my growth. They were considered 'sign posts', not teachers or guides. These sign posts initiated me into ways of learning growth and understanding that allowed me to harness my inner spiritual energy. After five years, I was fully developed and well beyond what any of them had expected me to accomplish. Upon completing this development, there were many things I was capable of achieving that were thought to be impossible for a mere mortal to accomplish. I was able to raise my vibration to a point where I could physically disappear. I was able to make plants grow out of rocks. I was able to tell them anything they desired to know of the future. I even went so far as to help a man grow back his amputated leg. I could make snakes appear and make hair grow on people's bodies where it had never grown before. They were speechless and frightened with this display of gifts for they believed I was to be their messiah but not a God. My energy, my insight and my love frightened them all.

At the age of 15, I moved back to Jerusalem and began travelling around the land talking to those who would listen. When I would meet strangers on the road, all I would say to them was "God is with you". They would then feel their own inner spirit; some were so moved they began to speak in tongues. This was a form of initiating them and assisting them into contacting their own God within and the reason for their quick transformation. For some, their bodies would come alive once they heard my words and they knew their way, their truth and their desires. However, only a few followed me.

I loved each of my disciples. Of the twelve, three were women who had changed their names and cut their hair to look as if they were male. John was Joan, Paul was Sarah and Bartholomew was Ruth. During my time, women were not given an equal voice. With me, however, women knew that their voice was equal to any other. The disciple I loved the most was the one who was the most challenged, Judas. Judas had visions of my death and knew his purpose well, yet, he tried desperately to change it. He was constantly tortured by the love and the hatred I seemed to evoke within him. Out of the twelve disciples Judas was the only one who had prophetic sight. He was the only one who could see what I saw but he could not bear to see them. Therefore, he constantly needed to run from me because he could not permit himself to be with me.

Following my death, only three of my disciples survived and the word of my crucifixion spread far and wide. What is now understood as the Bible is a compilation of different parts of my teachings before my death. Often, I would speak of the House of Job, the pharaohs or Moses and explain to those who listened the trials and tribulations of their ancestors. I would show them the mistakes and explain to them what God told Moses. Even though God spoke to Moses, Moses did not understand and it was only through blind faith that Moses was able to lead his people. There were many times Moses doubted what he was told from God. Each time he doubted, however, inevitably something would go wrong. His doubts were the doubts he inherited from his people.

You may question why women were often not recognized in the Bible's teachings. They were mentioned a great deal in the original text but with time, the names and the stories were changed to show men as befitting the voices of God, and the masses eventually believed that the voice of God could only come through a man.

God spoke often to women, especially to my mother Mary. Mary had great insight and vision but what is not commonly known is that she had no physical voice. She was unable to physically speak. The angels spoke to her often but her insightful gift remained hidden since she could not tell others about what she knew. Within Mary was a great deal of spiritual light and in giving birth to me, she knew well who I was but was unable to verbalize it.

At the time I was born, pregnancy took only three months from the point of conception to the time of delivery, but through evolution the period of pregnancy has lengthened since the vibration on your physical plane has slowed down. As angels appeared to me, my mother Mary also often appeared to children because children understood her light and her energy, and did not need speech to understand her. When children claim that Mary has appeared and spoken to them, it is not with words but with her energy that she speaks. I too was able to speak through my energy and I did not need to say much for people to understand me.

The Bible as it exists now is approximately one quarter of the teachings that were originally spoken; this is how people have wanted the Bible to be written. I broke the bread and shared the wine as described. The wine was the river of knowledge within me which symbolized the energy that poured through my blood, and those who shared my wine also shared my energy and my knowledge and became wiser for it. The breaking of bread was a ritual, a blessing to those who were with me in the room. It symbolized the nourishment of the soul and the coming together of everyone as one. It was a common spiritual ritual, however you wish to interpret it, that many undertook when coming together to pray or give thanks.

The Last Supper was a feast and Judas as well as myself subconsciously knew it would be our last meal together with all of the other disciples, but neither myself nor my disciples knew it would be the end. The Last Supper was a celebration. The twelve disciples represented the twelve nations of the world; and the thirteenth, which was myself, was considered the one who would bring all nations together as one. What transpired during my life is transpiring now and serves as a parallel for what will happen again in the future. For you to understand and know beyond the knowing, you first must learn to trust beyond the trusting.

"Yea, though I walk through the valley of the shadow of death" simply means that while I walk with those who are living, to me they are dead. "I shall fear no evil" means that there is no evil. Look beyond what you see to see through your blindness, and through your blindness you shall have sight.

May God's moment be ever eternal.

SESSION 6

My father Joseph was a carpenter but there were many other things he was capable of doing. Often, he travelled from village to village to help people fix things, and even though this work brought in little money it sufficed nonetheless. My father Joseph was a traveller who knew the land and the people who lived there quite well. To each place he travelled he heard news about many different events, plans, ideas and problems that were taking place. Joseph had a great deal more knowledge than most and educated himself through conversation. My father was a master of disguise and often times would travel inconspicuously.

When I was born my father did not believe for one moment that he was bringing a messiah into the world; he did not think that I was exceptional in any way. I was the second child, not the first as many assume; when Mary and Joseph travelled to Bethlehem to have me, they also had a two-year-old son with them. During that time people had few possessions, even those individuals who lived in their own dwellings had few possessions and little furniture.

Joseph wed Mary with the traditional expectations that she would be a good wife and mother for his children. She was by no means extraordinary except that her quietness and inability to speak made her stand out amongst all others. Wherever Mary travelled and whomever she was around, it was rare that she went unnoticed.

Considering the difficulties to survive that many families experienced at the time of my birth, Joseph and Mary were more fortunate than most. When I was born famine had already taken a large toll on the population and I arrived into the second year of a seven- year plight. For some reason, however, whenever food was scarce, a stranger or a traveller would arrive at our doorstep with food in hand. There was never an explanation for this but eventually my father realized that something unusual was taking place. My mother Mary, on the other hand, accepted the strangers much more graciously as if she understood why they had come. None of the strangers who arrived at our door ever stayed to eat the food they had left. They would come asking for directions and in turn for our kindness in providing information they would leave food behind.

By the age of three, I was able to communicate clearly with my mother. We spoke to each other through our thoughts. We had meaningful conversations through thought and wherever I travelled throughout my life, I could always hear my mother speaking to me in the back of my mind. At times she would call out to me and I would return the message. Rarely was my mother upset when I travelled because no matter where I went, she instinctively knew where I was and that I was fine.

The pain of my death was an unfortunate event she had to experience. From the period shortly before my birth until the time she had passed away, my mother carried many heavy thoughts concerning my purpose and my direction. Her only solace came through her ability to openly communicate with me through our thoughts. My mother and I had a unique connection unlike any other between mother and son, one she did not even share with Joseph.

Like myself, my mother Mary had come to this physical world with a purpose, but neither of us fully understood the outcome. She followed her thoughts and understood the weight they carried. Not until the age of five was I aware of her visions until I too began to see the visions she saw through our unique connection. When visions appeared to her, her mind would become quite still and she would observe what was before her. It took me a great deal of time to comprehend the quietness of her thoughts but once I understood them, I could understand what she was seeing.

Mary's visions came in the form of voices; they were explanations of who I was, why I existed and what I was to accomplish. Mary's purpose, unknown to her at the time, was to heal the multitudes, but because she was a simple woman of little means, she had little comprehension of how she could assist the masses. It was not clear to her when she was alive that even following her death the multitudes would call upon her for help and healing. Only when Mary died and resided in the metaphysical realm did she fully comprehend the visions and purpose of when she lived on earth. Mary was told when she was alive that she would alter the world through the teachings of Christianity and she played a significant role in changing people's lives through her guidance and quiet strength.

Strangely enough, however, my mother Mary did not believe in God. She believed that there was a voice beyond and whatever shape the voice took did not matter. In her youth, Mary's visions and insight did not require her to believe in a God. Only after my birth did people's idea of a God take shape. People have no real conception, image or feeling of God. That is one of the reasons why I was delivered as Jesus Christ. I was a small aspect of God taking form in your likeness, still human but with God's consciousness. I came to your world to give God's consciousness shape. I was manifested to enable people to have a God to pray to. My purpose was to be human first so that you could see the side of yourself that was also human, and Godly second since one does not exist without the other.

I now wish to talk about Satan. As yet, I have not expressed the reasons for Satan's existence. There are many who believe that the world is corrupt and evil as well as kind, compassionate and good. Some believe that a devil named Satan exists who was cast from the heavens above. There have been many stories written about Satan and Lucifer, some with more credibility than others. In my thoughts I never considered Satan to be evil, and even though I was tempted by Satan, it was not a temptation that could lure me to the depths of hell. Satan showed me the temptations of your physical world and what people wanted me to be. Satan was a messenger to show me the unkinder sides of myself and he provided knowledge of the darker side. Satan was once considered the Angel of Death. At one time because death was common due to plagues and sickness, it was seen as all-powerful and some assumed that in death evil spirits entered people's bodies and took them away into the night. Therefore, over time the belief in Satan's strength grew and Satan's ability to challenge God seemed progressively stronger. However, if God Himself was all-powerful and had created everything how is it that Satan could have such strength? Furthermore, why would God create such an evil monster to torture and betray His or Her own children?

There is an Angel of Life as there is an Angel of Death; both stand at the gates to the spirit world. The Angel of Life breathes life and breath into the soul being born into the physical world while the Angel of Death takes away the breath and life from the soul travelling into spirit. Just as you have day and night, you also have heaven and hell. All of your concepts, ideas and realities have two components that make up one whole. God created one world with two sides and any soul may use his or her energy to create 'evil' thoughts, ideas and actions, just as a soul may transform a dark side of himself or herself into something warm and loving.

For all of its recognized benefits and insight, Christianity has still greater knowledge, insight and growth to offer, but what it has provided it has also taken away. People believe what their hearts want them to believe. If you believe you can selfishly move forward by taking away from another person, you would recognize this other person as representing the part of yourself which is helping you to survive in a material world.

Your religion does not adequately show you the human side to life. It does not explain that to love means to sacrifice. If I can love all of the children in your world, would it seem likely that I could take one child and treat it more kindly than another simply because of the other child's race, colour or creed? You must give even if you think you will lose and through this loss you will be found. Although someone else may always appear to possess more, if you truly know that you have everything you need, then you have enough.

Many of my teachings were stripped from the Bible because I spoke too freely of people's capability to love one another. I explained that the churches were established for the people and not to lead them. It may appear to you now that many religions lead their people, but the only religion I followed came from within and I learned to listen to my own voice as you must also learn to listen to yours. I told people that they did not need to be herded together like cattle to listen to messages that told them of what they needed or had to do. I encouraged people to speak out and for a while many did. But each person is human and also susceptible to temptation. If you are tempted, you will not lose your soul, you will only learn from your temptations. If you are tempted and fall prey to your temptations, you are much wiser than those who never encounter this experience.

I am speaking through this soul, Dale Landry, but not in the words of the Bible according to Matthew, Luke or John or anyone else. I am simply speaking of what I know and if your ability to listen is attached to your heart, it will become a companion to your soul and you will know whether or not the words I speak fit your beliefs.

SESSION 7

I wish to speak about my own personal development. There are those individuals who saw me as a spiritual leader, who introduced the masses to a structured religion and created a pathway towards a greater understanding of myself and God. In your world, what the masses desire has sooner or later become mass-produced. In serving the multitudes many of my ideas were diluted and what was originally desired by people became lost into a sea of undecipherable information.

As an example, I was created to give people an avenue to find God but over time I was seen as God Himself. I was 'mass-produced' to make people believe that I could absolve them of their perceived sins and obstacles. What people perceived of me was in reality an image of what they desired me to be, not what I was. I never wished to be placed on a pedestal or praised as a God who could eliminate your difficulties; I cannot provide all the answers to prayers if you do not wish to answer them yourself. Throughout time I have stood out as the one solution to every problem.

God has created each individual in his or her own light as unique and unusual, but with similarities to everyone. The lessons to be learned are both simple yet so difficult to master. I loved everyone I came into contact with, including those who wanted to hurt me because I realized it was my responsibility to look beyond their limitations, that I was the one who needed to change in order to achieve my goals. I could perform miracles and change the way the world was viewed although I could not be what others expected.

To love unconditionally was my forte. I was capable of interacting with others without assuming them to be less or better than myself. Because of this gift, others in turn would approach me, feeling secure that I would not judge or think of them as undesirable.

Today you fear the judgement of others but what you do not clearly see is that other people's judgements are really your judgement of yourself. You have been taught to view the world through critical eyes and so the world has become a judgmental and unsavory place to be. If you inhabit this physical reality and you are worthwhile, then your companions share the same space and attitude as you do. Their approach may be different but their purpose will inevitably be the same as yours. It may appear simple to speak of love and forgiveness but if you encounter a difficult predicament, love and forgiveness are hard to feel.

As an institution the church in whatever form it takes teaches that only God is capable of forgiving you for your sins. However, the only true sin is committed when you deny love, compassion and forgiveness to yourself. To believe that God is capable of anger is to believe that God is harsh and unjust, and accordingly the God in your life will reflect the anger you project.

If religion is your God, then you must be a part of your religion and not live outside of it. It is your responsibility to make the decisions and not rely on an institution that remains outside of yourself. To be responsible for what you choose is to be responsible for your life and each decision therein. To allow others to decide for you what your God should be is to let your love, compassion and forgiveness slip through your fingers and fall unto a barren wasteland that will not produce the fruit you desire.

I do not criticize you for your beliefs or faith. I am merely showing you that each part of your life requires your own voice and you must listen to it. It is the voice of your heart to which you must focus. This is a part of your soul.

Your self-constructed prison confines you as I was also once confined. Some individuals are imprisoned for years or a lifetime, both justly or unjustly for speaking out against God, society and the norms of what you believe to be true. If each individual was responsible for his or her own life, there would be no need for institutions that require prisoners.

Many believe that it is wrong to set a prisoner free but to change this attitude does not occur overnight. Ironically, when your nation's leaders send your young off to war to die, is that not a capital offense itself—to sacrifice for the purpose of protecting oneself? If society did not believe in war, then it would not support the belief that many must die needlessly. It is not men or women who perpetuate war but a collective choice that society itself believes.

Human infirmity has always existed and it motivates many individuals to process change and rejuvenate their purpose in life. However, I do not see sickness as something necessary but something that should be condoned. Greed is a type of illness that keeps you isolated from your neighbour, a companion you believe you need to out-survive. If you act out of greed and aggressively choose to manipulate your physical circumstances and those around you, you will achieve what you only assume to be your inner desires. One's motivation for choosing greed may be as basic as survival or the need to look after those who are close to you. However, such base motives are self-perpetuating, just as would be your denial of what you are here to accomplish. To use the words 'right' or 'wrong' creates in your mind a belief that there is only one path to take in life; some take the right path and others the wrong.

I consider that my pathway was clear albeit confusing. In each moment I lived, regardless of the confusion within myself, my direction was clear. People believe that confusion stops you from clearly seeing your direction but if you look beyond the confusion, you will know well the direction you must take. Everyone shares a strong desire to know their career and purpose. I had no career but I did have a purpose which was to understand myself and assist those around me who were in some ways less fortunate. I have no doubt that the words I speak in this book will again in future be misconstrued. My words will be dissected and used as a defense by people who understand what I am saying but will use them to justify their own views that they are right.

One must understand my words in the context of the whole picture. In past you have been shown a Christ that was all knowing, totally forgiving and a victim of circumstance. But to look more closely you will see that I was the same as everyone else. I was human and no doubt gifted beyond what many of you will achieve but nevertheless I was still your equal. To assume that I am unattainable is to believe that your own Godhood is unattainable. If I stand out above everyone then I cannot possibly be a part of who you are. You will have many thoughts as you read these words, questions will arise and even more will remain.

You have your own ideas about my life but these thoughts lie within yourself and do not reflect the soul, Dale Landry, who I am speaking through; Mr. Landry is simply a conductor of my information. To continually ask yourself questions of your own heart and soul will reveal what you need to know about yourself. If you believe you have been forgotten and are disheartened by the abandonment of those who were supposed to love and protect you, fear not because you exist as I did to light the way for others. Take heed that there is purpose in not being recognized or sought after by the multitudes, and feel at peace knowing that although others may not seek you out, you are as capable as the greatest world leaders.

I do not want you to believe in damnation because that in itself will push you to believe that you must be good and find heart in the little means you have for survival. There is no good or bad, simply who and what you are. You are accountable for your actions to yourself and after passing from this physical reality, you will return once again to live out this accountability.

Many believe that when you die you stand before God in judgement. What happens initially is that you are released from the restrictions of your physical body so that you can attune yourself to the vibration of spirit and the movement of energy through thought. At that point, your understanding and concept of God broadens and you stand before a council of peers to address what you have accomplished; however, it is not a judgement. Picture yourself carrying a blueprint of your soul when you pass into spirit. You take that blueprint wherever you go and when you stand before the council you take a look at what you have learned in life. You then decide what you want to change and if there are more lessons you need to learn but did not from your last life. The council exists to advise, assist and help you understand how the blueprint of your soul works.

To broaden your thoughts and understanding of God is to expand your perception and understanding. You acknowledge the parts of yourself that are God just as those who stand before you are both separate yet a part of you that is God. Imagine God as one ball of light made up of many different particles. If you were to remove one of the particles, it would reduce the intensity of light just as it would reduce that which makes up God. You are an important part of that huge ball of light and together, with all other individuals, you form an unconscious collective that propels itself forward through a mass of time which you consider as eternity. However, in reality, there is no eternity and no time, simply the existence of what is and shall be.

It is difficult to comprehend that only one thing really exists when your teachings tell you the exact opposite. You may ask why does God not intervene and show you the path and direction? The answer is simple; it is your responsibility to listen to your own voice within to discover your path. To deny that voice within is to deny your life. Until such a time when the collective unconscious can create a harmonious existence, there will always be death, destruction and pain as you experience it.

Your purpose is to create a harmonious existence in a physical world that feels empty without God. However, you only see God as an illusion in your physical reality because you have created a God that appears outside of yourself when in truth you harbour God within yourself. To use your heart as a gateway to heaven, you first must pass through hell to get there; the heart contains the physical and spiritual vibrations and you must first pass through the physical world to achieve the spiritual. You may believe that the pathway towards the spiritual vibration is simple, however, learning only comes through patience which in itself has a high price that many feel is and of itself a living hell.

SESSION 8

When I addressed the masses, my words and methods of speech varied often and rarely did I present my teachings in the form of questions. Many individuals simply came to listen while others sought to understand their purpose. I often spoke of the Old Testament of the Bible, the lives of their ancestors, Moses and their purpose. It was of the utmost importance that the people I spoke to understood why they were afflicted with such pain, sorrow, poverty and disease. They sought answers to their afflictions that no one else was capable of providing. Many people had heard my name from far and wide and they travelled long distances to find me. Even the children who came sat quietly while I spoke. The energy that I emitted was peaceful, serene, insightful and healing to those who sat with me. Many would lose their aggressive tendencies and seek instead to find solutions to their problems.

Moses led his people to the Promised Land and provided them with the Ten Commandments to live by; I have spoken of each commandment and their purpose. The Ten Commandments provided a structure to show people how to love. They were not rules and regulations as a prison but over time they have evolved into such a paradigm.

Love thy neighbour as thyself simply means that if you love and care for yourself, you will naturally respect others and love them for who they are.

Thou shalt not commit adultery. At the time this was written, men were allowed many wives and while it was not that such an idea was considered wrong, it was necessary to show that in some situations women were being neglected, unloved and left as unwanted. Therefore, this commandment was written to show people their propensity towards greed and to help them realize the importance of concentrating on one thing at one time. To have too many wives was similar to having too many slaves and women at that time were treated

35

as slaves. The commandment served to free women from their slavery.

Thou shalt not covet thy neighbour's goods. At the time this was written it was not uncommon to scheme to outdo others who were perceived as having more. Thus, the way to survive for many involved taking from others. This commandment demonstrated how each person needed to understand the importance of sharing and assisting each other.

Thou shalt not steal. It was important then as it is now to respect each individual's material goods and not to deny another for what he or she has worked for. To steal is to harm. You can steal someone's heart just as easily as you can steal someone's goods. To steal is to take from yourself and project your feelings of loneliness and pain onto another person.

I am Lord and God, thou shalt not be false Gods before me. In the pagan religion it was not uncommon to make sacrifices. These sacrifices were not harmful if the food was utilized thereafter for the people. However, what often happened is that the animals were needlessly sacrificed to appease the Gods above for whatever perceived reason. The flesh of the animal would then be left to waste. Thus, this commandment promised a more humanitarian side to life which required instilling the idea of prayer to one God and eliminating the need to sacrifice the few possessions people had.

When I spoke to people, I would explain how I had come to gain my knowledge. I would answer their questions even before they asked and I would tell them that they had little to fear but fear itself. Fear was common since many believed that they would be sacrificed for penance or for some type of wrong-doing. At that time, penance was required by all and you gave your hard earnings to the state in this regard. Those that hid their earnings were tortured and sometimes put to death. The masses were kept poor, ignorant and uneducated. They had no way out of their dilemma except through death.

I often spoke about the many changes to come in the future and explained that God heard their cries of anguish and would help them out of their difficulties. I explained to them that there were lands beyond their borders that had not yet been discovered; lands that were fertile and rich. Some listened, but most did not. The barren lands I spoke of were part of the Promised Land, the place where their ancestors had settled.

Everyone believed it was their purpose to live in the Promised Land, but when Moses led his people there, it was not the Promised Land they thought it would be. The land where they settled was however a place of freedom and a way out of the despair they had experienced...The Promised Land that God spoke of was simply a description that incorporated the ideas of the skies above and the earth below that would provide for all to exist. It provided a solution for people to discover more about themselves and learn why each soul incarnated...The Promised Land was wrongly interpreted by Moses as a specific location or area.

The fighting still continues within the Promised Land and if this is supposedly God's sacred place one would wonder why it is in such turmoil. Why do people fight over a piece of dirt that is barren and provides little fruit or vegetation? Why do these protagonists not understand that the land they fight over will still be there long after they are gone? Why do these people fight over things that will bring them no benefits?

Moses fought for his people but in the end he was discouraged at what he discovered. He had foreseen the ensuing war. For this reason, Moses did not venture forth so willingly into the Promised Land simply because he understood its destiny. Moses and his people were discouraged as I too was discouraged and broken hearted when I reached my final demise, but not because I had been wronged and put to death, but because the longing within my heart begged for peace on earth.

I frequently explained to the multitudes my visions of the wars and the famines that would occur in later years and that many of their offspring would also grow and prosper and spread the word of God. When I spoke of God I spoke of the Divine energy within each and every soul and everything that exists. I explained that it is pointless to envy your brother or sister because all souls and creatures are a part of you. My words were not always understood, but on an intuitive level people who listened believed me.

Ironically, my people, the Jewish people, still believe that I have not yet come, that their King has not yet arrived; the Christians, however, who were not my people, see that I have. Interestingly, while the Christians did not fully understand my purpose, they were quite willing to follow.

As I have mentioned already, there will not be a Second Coming as many believe and I will not return as Jesus Christ. I will avail myself to the more human side of life, more likely as a female, to show you that there is no superior race or gender but to show you that you are human and one important element in the sparkle of God's Divine light.

Over time you will discover that the walls that keep you enclosed— your beliefs, attitudes and your approach to life will each dissolve as you are brought back to the oneness known as God.

Of ashes to ashes and dust to dust, God's breath is in all that exists such as the breath within you, the air around you, the wind and the trees of nature, the birds that sing, the animals that roam the earth and the seas that we swim. To find God you must use your senses, especially the one known as your heart.

SESSION 9

When I was young and still learning, the angels revealed many things to me. I constantly received messages throughout my life and although they came in many different forms, as I have said, they were most commonly received through the voices of angels. At other times, I would experience visions as a result of the words of strangers, friends and children. One time, in particular, I sat alone in a cave and felt it important to express certain ideas in order to receive messages. The words I used were of this nature:

With spirit before my eyes, I allow myself to be revealed and to understand the workings of my soul. In the face of my creator, all is safe now and ever shall be.

The words are so simple but I was moved enough that I recommend you also use them. The message I received follows this affirmation. If you understand that time stands still, that nothing moves forward or back and that as a collective force we all exist as one light, you will understand who or what your master, God, or the light within, truly is. Imagine a kaleidoscope and the many beautiful colours that exist within it. Each colour is an expression of all living creatures that exist, have existed or will live in the future.

To find one's path is not easy. Ask for your purpose to be revealed through your own light and allow the answer to form as it may. Words carry a certain vibrational sound but are also an expression of thought. When you send out that thought, there is a colour and form it takes and in turn the answer will carry with it a similar light and colour. To discover the answers to difficult questions, there is another affirmation to present while in quiet meditation or prayer.

Release me master from the baggage that this life carries and assist my eyes to know what it is I desire to understand. Take care the gentle thoughts that return to my heart, that the key to my soul turns gently and that I know it is Your hand which will unlock all there may be.

I learned at a young age the value of gentleness. I was taken out by my father on an excursion where we came upon an animal that was wounded and dying. My father said to me, "If you were this animal, how would you desire to be treated before death?" I had no words, only emotions and feelings that went beyond what I was able to express. My father said, "All who come here whether physically healthy or not are wounded, so it is important to learn to treat everything and everyone with the same care."

It was then that I understood the meaning of life was death and that all things, albeit alive and vibrant, were simultaneously dying. Later as I thought about the wounded animal and how I would want to be treated if I lay dying, I would desire love, compassion and a warm heart. Pride and dignity, although considered to be important in death, are only obstacles to reaching the end. When one finds his or her release in death, their soul will breathe a new life and a new awareness, one that takes on a new approach to the master. I use the word 'master' not to indicate one who is superior since together we are each our own masters.

During my life I saw the master as having great knowledge, understanding and experience that evolved with time and maturity. We are each masters of our own universe and the creators of all that we see. Together, we form what you know as God.

In speaking through this soul, Dale Landry, I am taking my time to form the thoughts I wish to express. There is no need to hurry myself along because by the time I finish my work I will enjoy what I have created in each moment. When I travelled throughout my life, I never hurried to get from one destination to another. For me, time occurred within the moment, and each moment occurred within another moment. If you take your time and put one step in front of the other, and do it slowly, gradually as you watch your feet go, you will discover that time does not exist and that each step is simply the same moment repeated. This is how I characterize living in the moment.

Imagine yourself walking on air, unable to progress forward, yet watching your feet move; no matter how far you have travelled you still end up at the point where you began. As such, by running away from your troubles you discover that they still remain regardless of how far you have travelled. In essence, you remain at the point where you began.

Only once did God appear to me in my life. It was the day before my death when I saw the skies above opening up my mind. As my mind opened up a voice said unto me "Jesus, you are my child. Wherever you are, I am there. Go in peace."

In that moment I realized that a large part of my mission had been accomplished. I realized that I had come as a missionary of peace and despite my insightfullness, I was still unaware of what lay before me. There were so many people that sought my advice, including teachers who asked me to speak to their pupils and healers who wanted to replicate my abilities. But to all of these fellow seekers I would say; "Go in peace and know that God is with you." Often, they were perplexed with my response because they believed that I was their God, or at least an expression of Him. They could not recognize that they also possessed the same knowledge.

At times I felt defeated to be amongst so many who could not see or hear what I could. I felt isolated throughout my life because I had answers that others could not see. And although I had the insight and peace within my heart, I walked alone amongst the numerous souls who did not realize who I truly was. My loneliness increased as even the wisest of individuals could not understand my way of thinking or what I said. When I spoke, I would explain the messages I had received from the angels but they did not understand me as I had expected they would. The people I talked to could feel the words I spoke and although I knew I told the truth, I did not know how my words were interpreted to the people and where it would take them. As a result, I was perplexed since the masses believed that I spoke in riddles even though I presented the information as it was told to me. To me, the angels' language was simple but to all others it was complex.

Although I knew that the masses did not understand me, I held firmly in my belief of self existence. I saw purpose in what I had to say, and knew that in the end my words would become clearer. My ascension into heaven was viewed by those who had joined me in death as God taking back His son. But what it truly represented was the process of a

41

soul leaving its physical body and environment to become light since it no longer required a body to carry. Through its lightness, a soul returns to the source from which it came and elevates upwards towards God. To understand that you have the gift of life is to actualize the breath of God in your physical existence. When that gift ends, you are lifted upwards from whence your soul came.

SESSION 10

In my youth I believed that God was all wonderful and all giving, who saw and knew everything. When I reached the age of 13, I pondered greatly my surroundings and the people I met. I questioned the idea that if God could hear and see everything, and knows everyone's problems, why was there so much despair? I also questioned my own loneliness and although I knew that God existed, I was puzzled as to my purpose. I pondered what the purpose of such loneliness in life would accomplish for me when I passed away? One evening the Archangel Michael spoke to me; I boldly asked these questions, wondering if he was capable of giving a satisfactory answer. His reply was bewildering and left me perplexed for the following two years. He simply replied that all living things on earth manifested the earth itself and that the concept of God existed to keep everyone progressing and moving forward. He explained that there were many different worlds, each formed through different expressions of thought. He spoke of four worlds in particular, including the earth, each materialized from the source known as God. He explained that our life purpose is complicated and intertwined within these three other worlds. He also showed me that the physical body is made up of energy and physical material created from earth. For instance, by eating the trees and plants and other living creatures, all animals including humans contain the ability to reproduce. Therefore, every living thing survives on the elements that come from earth.

The soul, however, comes from an intangible world and carries with it a purpose that makes each soul unique. All souls are linked together by a common cause and come from a world beyond the metaphysical, a world of simple energy that produces thought. And beyond this world is the pure form known as God who creates the images of humankind in His likeness. Therefore, the manifestation of man, woman and child are each elements of a material world that mirror a place not quite physically tangible to us, yet still within our reach.

I understand that this information may appear somewhat confusing at first. In the simplest terms, we exist to create an image of ourselves to reflect a physical likeness of God, to understand our intangible side and to express our purpose which is the part we know as God.

Our attempt to perfect our race is also a reflection of what occurs in the metaphysical and physical worlds as energy, thought and image are themselves constantly recreated and perfected. We exist to learn that there is no space, no time and no fear, but only that which is imagined. As we persist in our efforts to confront the deepest of our fears, we in turn create a more harmonious and more satisfying existence on every level of our souls.

Imagine your own personal world where the sun is the source of life, the air and sky as the energy to support your existence, the surface of the water as thought and the depths of the ocean as the physical essence in which you are created. In the depths of the ocean there is great pressure from above to survive. This is felt from each of the higher levels, and the intensity is stronger and more pronounced as you move downwards. As you change and evolve you move higher towards the surface of the water where the pressure becomes lighter. Finally, as you break the water's surface, you pass into spirit and grow wings like a bird that flies higher into the new reaches of the skies with a greater view of all that exists below. Then as a sphinx propelled into the sun, you are burned and consumed by the brightness of the sun's light which is the very core of what gives breath to life.

In response to Michael's interpretation, I asked one final question; "Why do we experience such turmoil and pain if only to learn lessons? And if we come from such a highly evolved source, why do we need to live on earth?" He replied, "Even God needs to know that He exists and so the evolution of humankind is to know that within all of us, God exists. And although the sun resides high above us, without it, we cannot survive."

SESSION 11

John the Baptist facilitated many individuals who looked for me, the Messiah. Without his preachings, developed beliefs and insightful visions, people would not have known who I was. Some believed that John the Baptist himself was the Messiah because his preaching was so forceful and clear sighted. John the Baptist often spoke of his many visions and he knew exactly who I, Jesus Christ, was. Many people wanted him to lead but John the Baptist knew his path well including his demise. He was, however, blinded by faith and drive and could think of nothing else but his people's freedom. At that time there was no middle ground as one searched for a path of understanding or was lost in darkness. There were two occasions when I met John the Baptist, once at age 13 during my studies and later that year at the river of baptism.

The purpose behind the ritual of baptism was not to release people from their sins but to cleanse them, allow them to start anew and to give them faith. Baptism is a method of demonstrating to each human and each soul that they are recognized in the moment and that each moment is their own. To some, rituals mean very little and to others it is an important way of life. One does not need rituals to survive but they may serve as a meaningful structure for many; it provides both purpose and momentum. To say to your husband, wife, partner or loved one each day that you love them instills purpose, commitment and communication as well as the recognition that you are joined together.

Much like myself, when John the Baptist died, he was released from a very difficult and challenging life, although it was one of tremendous purpose. And even though he appeared as an exceptional figure at the time, history has acknowledged him as someone who believed and was committed to his life purpose. The rituals of your ancestors have been lost and now you are trying to formulate a purpose of your own. Thus, it is important to understand your purpose from a view point that is important to you. To go through the motions of living without any real purpose is very much like trying to drive a vehicle without gas.

You likely believe that there are far too many people in the world for you to feel important enough to have purpose, however, that is only an excuse one uses to try not to discover what their purpose really is. Living from day-to-day, from moment-to-moment and simply not existing to one's potential is a pattern people played out when I lived and so history is repetitive. Education has done little to give you an awareness or an ability to think. You must utilize your own innate knowledge and unlock the key to your heart and soul. To find your voice, first you must realize you have a voice to find.

At the time of my birth there were many differing beliefs about religion and different Gods, as well as a great deal of pressure such as you have now to follow one leader. I did not look to lead; I wanted to show by example how many could live. But to lead is to show by example and I was placed in this position of being something that I was not, which was a God, a king, a ruler and a leader. To this day, I am still seen in such a light and therefore kept distant from you until such a time where you can set an example for yourself and lead your own life through your own existence.

It has been speculated with uncertainty that I was asexual. I was seen as androgynous and as a leader who did not desire intimate companionship. However, during the years that I travelled I learned that my sexuality and sexual energy could be used to help me in my growth and could also heal people. Because my sexual energy was directed towards healing people, the masses experienced and interpreted this energy as Holy. And this is why I was perceived as androgynous

I had intimate relationships but the Bible has not recorded them. The Bible does not speak of the human side of Jesus Christ because that would take away from my power and I would no longer stand out above the rest. It is presumed that if I was so weak in flesh I could not possibly have been the son of God or if my mother was not a virgin how could I possibly have been so gifted? Some issues were obviously measured incorrectly.

The Bible tells you that I was human but also the son of God, and uncharacteristic to others who are also said to be the sons and daughters of God. I did not shine more brightly than you. I simply understood my purpose. To believe without thought is to live without life; to question without thinking is like thinking without a question; and to fly without wings is to die without breath. I am amongst you although only a few of you see me and even fewer believe.

By the year 2010, formalized religion as you know it will no longer exist. Even now, however, many still believe that there is a need for rituals although they do not follow them. To meditate without understanding why serves little purpose. Asking God for forgiveness when you do not know why you need to be forgiven serves little purpose if there is no real sin to be removed. I will reiterate that you must challenge every aspect of your belief system. You must understand the logic behind my sarcasm, whether the information I speak of in this book is true to you and why I have returned to speak to you. Asking why is a very important question but you must also take the time to search for the answer.

I believe that in your life Charles[4] all things are doubtful. You question all that is before you and trust nothing, yet you say that you do believe. As you sit here today, deep in the recesses of your thoughts, you doubt as others do that it is I, Jesus Christ, who has come to speak. And even if I stood before you in my robes and you finally did believe I was here, others would not believe you and would consider you to be irrational and of questionable character. To believe, you must first think because if you do not think you do not live and if you do not live, you exist without purpose. The multitudes that I spoke to lived without purpose just as you live without purpose. Only with time, when the thunder bolt releases its flash from above will the mind, the heart and the soul open to recognize their purpose.

4Charles is a student of the instrument, Dale Landry, who sat with Dale during this session. In this paragraph, Jesus Christ, through Dale, has directed his attention for the moment towards Charles.

SESSION 12

The arrival of the year 2000 is similar to the time period of around my birth. It will bring many great changes that you are already experiencing physically, environmentally, spiritually and emotionally. Throughout history, there were many diseases that plagued the multitudes, and afflictions of the body will always exist to help people grow and advance spiritually. During the time I visited the sick, there were many theories as to the reasons for one's physical ailments, much like there are today, and there was a common belief that there was no cure for illness. So many gave up hope, thinking that there was no way to change or to find physical health.

I will offer another affirmation which you can use to change your physical well being. Be aware, however, that the changes you will experience will not occur as you may assume. If you are suffering from a disease such as cancer, it is a common belief that without medical attention you will quickly perish. What I suggest is for you to follow your heart for what you believe is the best avenue for healing yourself. Do not see your affliction as a hindrance. Listen quietly to what the disease has come to teach you and see it as an opportunity to release the anger of your past, the pain of your youth or the distress of your present predicament. You may repeat the following each morning and each evening, or as many times as you choose:

> I release unto myself the light that will erase my pain and bring me to full strength, health, balance and harmony in all areas of my life.

I am not suggesting that this affirmation will heal you, stop the progression of illness or even prevent you from passing away. What I am saying is that you have an intuition—a voice within that can provide answers and you are capable of healing yourself in many different forms. I did not heal nor make anyone better who did not desire to be healed. Furthermore, I did not remove anyone's pain; I simply showed them the way.

Many people call out searching for answers as to why their lives feel so unfulfilling. It is not that riches do not surround you or are not abundant, it is simply that you cannot see them and cannot open your heart to enjoy the simple pleasures of life's gifts like the people who love you. As I stated earlier, many have tried to emulate me but no one has tried to be me. The difference of course is that people are hesitant as to whether they want to own their voice within as I owned the voice that I possessed.

Throughout the centuries most if not all people have been skeptical of what they see before them; they believe God does exist because this is what they have been told to think, but they are unclear as to their resolve. However, it is one thing to believe what you are told and another to believe because of what feels right for you. Most people learn to act out their parent's ideals of perfection, happiness and achievement. One strives to be placed on a pedestal and accomplish what no other has yet achieved. One soon realizes, however, that the view from above is not one of contentment but one of sorrow, pain and loneliness as one becomes out of reach to others. I stood on that pedestal although it was my desire to live amongst the multitudes, but the more I tried the farther out of reach I became.

My existence as Christ was paradoxically complex, yet simple. Loneliness was both my number one companion and my challenge. I was always faced with the shadow of death on one side, the shadow of loneliness on the other, the light of God before me and an unrecognized past behind me. Wherever you face, you will see north to your front, south to your back and so forth. The north is where you will long to be, the south is the light of your past and the east and west are the rights and wrongs you believe exist to guide you. You can symbolize the east and west as your mother and father, the north as your God and the south as your devil. Where they cross is the centre and within that centre is included hell, heaven and yourself, but the only way towards emancipation is directly upwards, not north, south, east or west.

Each day you seek solutions to your problems. You request, demand and desire a way out of the conflicts in your life that appear unending; learn to take hold of the moment, seize the past, capture the future and release yourself through your own means. No one can help you unless you help yourself and no one can ease the torment unless you first ask for help. You may not believe in your heart that anyone can help you out of your despair but if you ask the answers will manifest.

For the gambler who forever believes that a windfall will release him from the pains of his life has the constant belief that with one big win he will receive his reward and all his prayers will be answered. Ironically, the answer may be to strip the gambler of everything he has in order that he discover all that he truly has, because once stripped of everything one is left to their own devices. The real desire of gamblers is to rid themselves of everything they have accomplished in order to find true happiness. So, by losing his family, a house, a job and friends, a gambler will create a challenge in his life which is either total failure or a success at beating the odds once again—which is another gamble.

You, as everyone, are a gambler striving for the ultimate jackpot of social acceptance and unconditional love. You mirror my torment, my pain and my loneliness although I tried to show people the way out of this when I lived. At the time, I did not perceive that I was not showing my followers a way out but rather a way in.

My physical death was painful and left the message that death is a frightening, punishing experience. But death is a form of rebirth which allows you to understand the different aspects of yourself that are unconscious to you while you are alive. You do not find all of your answers in death, just as you do not find all the answers in life. But in life or death, all the answers do lay before you.

The reasons for God's existence, your purpose and who you are, goes beyond the realm of life and death to a plane of existence known as 'anareria'—a world of vibration where you utilize your sense of awareness to know what is beyond All That Is or All That Exists. To get there, ask to be taken and eventually you will reach it. It is not required that you leave your physical body to travel there and there are no requirements of meditation or prayer; only the desire is required.

To look outside of yourself for answers is like looking for love where it does not exist. If you have a heart which is shut off from providing love to you, how will you be capable of knowing or understanding it when you draw it in? If your heart has no voice then there will be no response.

The words I speak in this book will be analyzed and spoken of in the years to come but few will truly utilize them. I could describe the words in your language as a 'happening thing' but nothing is really happening if it is not coming from within. If I put on dark glasses to deflect the sun would I not miss the reflection within your eyes which relays the message of your soul and tells me your heart is interested in mine?

Most people will do almost anything for love but will not do enough to change themselves. So, if you do not change how can you possibly allow yourself to feel love? Should you find yourself stationary in time, in one place, and the light is not shining upon you, would it not be a good idea to change your position and find a place where you and the light will meet? Or would you wait a whole day and night for the sun to return again to shine upon the one spot that you were standing on?

SESSION 13

Miracles happen every day but few people believe it, therefore I will further elaborate and define what a miracle is.

It is commonly believed that I changed water into wine and created bread and fish from nothing, certain miracles of sorts. To manifest what it is you truly desire in one moment is to create a new vibration in the same moment. This new vibration is the thought of that which you wish to manifest, and it is also how you can create a miracle.

To create a miracle, firstly you must realize you can do it; secondly, you must know it can be materialized; and thirdly, use your energy to manifest it. To achieve a miracle, the body uses its energy to initially absorb information and then it conducts this energy outward in order to manifest the miracle. Therefore, as you receive from the left, you manifest with the right. Your body and soul is attuned to achieving constant harmony; yin and yang. The miracle is not in what you manifest but in your capability to successfully use your energy to achieve your miracle. It may take ten to fifteen years to achieve it but with constant work and focus, it can happen. The miracles I created were given to help people change their own energy in order to manifest their own miracles. I was the key to unlocking the door for all individuals to personally discover the answers we are each seeking.

After the year 2000, the energy of this planet will change considerably and many new areas will open up to humans such as energy transference and energy manifestation. The positive side to this change is that you will learn to communicate in ways never before possible. The hazardous down side is that some individuals will misuse these newly found skills through greed and selfishness. I will not tell you how to discover these new fields because if it is something you truly desire, it shall come. To master these skills would take approximately 5 to 15 years, but if you misuse this energy you will become embroiled in a state of chaos for many lifetimes to follow. So take heed of my words. Pontius Pilot did not have me put to death because he feared my revenge. The truth is when he looked at me I mirrored back to him what he thought of himself. As wise as he was, he let the people choose my fate when in reality it was not their fate to choose since destiny itself held the card for my demise.

You believe in every moment that life, the world, your parents, God and the people around you owe you something. You hold onto the belief that you are less fortunate, no matter how hard you try to climb the social ladder to achieve fame and success. You look to God for answers but never listen closely to hear whether there is a voice answering back. You turn instead to the church and religious dogma filtered down through the centuries which only carry hollow verses and empty ideas. You expect that during your lifetime somehow the chaos and the confusion which surrounds you will end however it never appears to. You see the younger generation begin to make their mark and speed forward as eagerly as you did. The young think they can rectify the problems of their elders, but they find that the solutions are not so easily achieved and the pathway is much steeper than expected. Such confusion results when the answers come from outside of yourself and not from what you truly believe in your heart.

Pope John Paul is viewed as the highest symbol in Roman Catholicism yet the words he speaks centre around blasphemy. Never has a woman been able to hold such a position and speak about her needs. It is a lack of balance and harmony that you accept because you have been conditioned to believe it. To this day my words from the Bible are still used to oppress the multitudes which is in direct opposition to the message I meant to relay. Your world is imprisoned and you are herded like cattle into a fenced area. You believe that the pen is mightier than the sword but as books gradually become extinct, what will you view as mightier?

If women no longer feel that men should make decisions about their bodies, thoughts and beliefs, they should create their own churches. However, to progress in this direction, women must not fall prey to the ignorance that can so quickly destroy what good can result when people come together as one collective thought. The purpose in my idea is not to build bigger and better religious temples but to work together in the belief and understanding that God lies within. People come together to share, talk, laugh and cry; you do not need thousands to gather together to show how powerful God's words are. Who can truly know God's words if he or she does not listen?

Four friends who met once a week to discuss their lives, what they were doing and then to share food would be much farther ahead than the thousands who flock to an empty sermon of words meant for those who do not wish to see or hear. God only wants to know that you are linked with others, growing as a child striving to accomplish and discover what lies within. You have lost your comradary with others and there is no longer the same trust in your brother or sister. You seek to destroy instead of mending and to kill instead of talking. You attempt to unravel a problem by finding another one and in the end you discover only defeat.

If these words appear hollow or false then I need not say more for the reflection will be clear.

Men do not rule the world any more than a prisoner is truly imprisoned. If you feel jailed, set yourself free.

SESSION 14

During a particular lifetime I had before Christ, and prior to the time of Atlantis, I lived in northern Russia where the weather in that region was quite the opposite to what it is now. Most of the time it was extremely hot with desert-like conditions. In that lifetime, I was part of a large group of Nomadic people who were not ordinary voyagers but travelled mainly by means of levitation. During this lifetime, I was taught by my parents to use my thoughts to materialize and dematerialize objects. With this ability, I was also capable of travelling great distances. But, unlike others in the group, I quickly developed to a point where I could dematerialize my body and appear in a different land simultaneously. I was the only one in the group who held this ability because of the density of my vibration. Over time, there were only two others who were capable of this skill and of teaching it. They unsuccessfully attempted to teach it to others but this skill remained dormant. However, these other two souls have reincarnated and maintained this ability in your physical reality as I had also kept it in my lifetime as Jesus Christ.

The time that existed before Atlantis is not recorded in your history and even the existence of Atlantis is considered fictional to most as there is little proof of its existence. Throughout your many lifetimes you have sought the key to unlocking the mysteries of your past lives and your future purpose. What you do not see, however, is the wealth of information that is stored within the many lifetimes where you have travelled and learned so much. The reason you forget these lifetimes is because you believe that knowing about your past lives may hinder your soul's progress. In past, living souls knew about their past lives. The difficulty was that in having knowledge of the past life, the soul would feel greater commitment to their past experiences and was therefore hindered in progrssing forward. Even now, people still focus on their youth and their past in order to make sense of the future. When you begin to understand the greater context of your life and your purpose, you will see life as more rewarding.

Your life is not about being at the top of the social ladder. What is important is how you use your mind, your energy, your thoughts, your heart and the energy that lies within. In conjunction with the soul's motivation and the forward propelling motion of your physical body, you are then capable of unlocking many doorways. Develop a purpose that goes beyond the mundane. See yourself as striving towards the ability to project your thoughts into spirit while your body remains in the physical world. In doing so, you can levitate yourself or render a physical object weightless. Consider the possibilities of five to ten people gathering together to use their energy to make a sick person healthy and vibrant once again.

Humankind has spent the last 2000 years discovering its physical world and now it is being released from that world into a pure energy form. In the years ahead, as early as ten to fifteen years, you will be less likely to categorize your existence as you do now. Categories have the tendency to limit you. For instance, from the time you were young, if you were labelled as an accountant when inwardly your desire was to be a mechanic, you would never have believed that you could have achieved purpose or contentment. In this moment, you can begin the process to free yourself and release the shackles that bind you. There will always be people who are skeptical of my words and who feel that inner purpose and happiness is not possible. However their skepticism is rooted in a fear that others are more gifted, and by hindering others from moving forward, they will not have to deal with their fear of being left behind. In your desire to move forward, do not believe that you have to manifest your gifts outwardly. Instead, trust your heart that you know your pathway is unfolding. This information may appear confusing or you may feel you are incapable of achieving your desires. However, if you truly believe this in your heart, you will ultimately achieve your desired path.

In my lifetime in Russia, I was not a leader nor did I stand out as someone special. I was unique only in terms of my ability to dematerialize at will and I was taught to freely show others what I was capable of just as they taught me other things I did not know. In the life that I lived as Jesus Christ, I was not a quick learner. I was methodical and slow to formulate my thoughts into speech. I tried not to criticize others for fear that I would be criticized myself. Throughout my many lifetimes, I have concentrated heavily on my communication skills relying on the appropriate souls who have taught me well in this area.

In a lifetime I had before Christ and before Atlantis, I was taught the ability of foresight, to see into the future. I was also taught that regardless of what I saw, my visions could not impact my future. Just as each moment exists in the moment, the future cannot be changed. Just as this book was written and you are reading it now, you are experiencing what was written. You can alter your fate after what you have read in this book but altering your fate does not impact on what was written. There are so many variations of what the future can and will be in the moment. To decide tomorrow that you will have good physical health does not change your time of death but the decision does change the quality of your life. Therefore, within your own set of parameters, one always has ample   opportunity.

In the next number of years, as the structure of your society begins to collapse and as the poor become poorer and the rich seek to protect themselves, people will experience a great revelation and renewal of understanding and purpose that did not exist before. To perceive yourself as 'rich' is to be blind if you do not share your riches to help others since you will become less fortunate than those with little means. Each and every person is incredibly gifted but they need to share his or her gifts to understand their purpose. With love, I have come here to share.

SESSION 15

It is too simplistic to ask God to explain why we are here on earth since without proper experience or perception we are often unclear and misunderstand Him. God is present in all that we do, see, feel, believe and understand. If you took a moment to listen closely and ask if God exists, the reply would quickly come in the affirmative. There is no need for any other answers in life because once you know and understand that you are not alone you can begin to resolve your problems and challenges. Often people ask why God allowed them to be born sick or why God has allowed His children to pass away. Understand that, like people, not every flower or tree grows to its full potential and many individuals are harvested long before they reach their maturity. You may wonder why God has allowed this or you may just assume that it is part of life's cycle. Know that everyone and everything is unique and different, although there is a common thread that binds everything together. To understand life's cycle, first understand your own cycle of life, your own evolution and the reason why you exist. You will not find the answer if you do not ask yourself the questions. And while many questions may remain unanswered, most of the important ones will be understood and resolved long before your death—if you persist.

The solutions to poverty, disease and inequality are not money. The answers lie within you. As you learn compassion and the ability to know yourself and others, miracles will occur. The seed grows into a flower and will willingly offer its fragrance and beauty as it rejoices in its purpose. With time, you too can learn to rejoice in your purpose and what you have to offer, and express yourself to your fullest potential. It will not matter who is there looking on, telling you that you are beautiful. It will be your own voice within which will bring out your beauty and satisfy your hunger. The hunger that pushes you forward to manifest and realize your miracles is the hunger that seeks satisfaction and answers. However, if you misuse your desires you will discover heartache, discontent and disillusionment which will start you on a downward spiral of self-pity and demise.

Once when I travelled on a road to Bethlehem, I met an elderly man who due to his years and experience was truly wise. He asked me where I was going and although he was travelling in the opposite direction, he asked if he may walk with me. Clearly, he had never encountered such light and energy as my own and wanted to investigate and know more about it to satisfy his hunger. He did not fear that I would refuse to walk with him, but simply hoped that I would not object to his company.

Along our journey, we spoke little but said everything that needed to be said and when we parted, he simply replied that he would look for me again in his travels. And with that response I knew that should we meet again, he would recognize me by my light and had better understood his purpose.

My lifetime as Jesus Christ was to provide purpose to each soul on earth and to show the full potential of life. People, however, still fight and cry out for more, believing they want love when in reality they deny it and stay blind to it.

Looking back throughout history, many ask if I have accomplished a great deal since my death or if any real change of consequence has occurred? To most, I am perceived as an exceptional and unique leader of the multitudes, however, so was Martin Luther King as well as others throughout history. So, to what do I owe the honour and status as the son of God?

If I was as many would believe, why are so many religions which use my name today so corrupted? Why will no one follow in my footsteps and learn to be humble before a God that is viewed as precious? Why is it that each of you drink the water of life but constantly thirst? Why do you think that God, myself or others need to appear before you to prove that we exist? If you exist and are truly gifted, why do you doubt my existence at all?

Unlike any other time in history, you are moving into a period when there will be no religious leaders to guide you because as they will soon discover their purpose is not to merely preach the word of God. What will happen to the masses when you are left to your own devices? Will you shrink away and die of fear because there is no one there to lead you or will you take control of your voice and heart within and lead yourself out of your darkness into a brilliant light that can feed your hunger?

Too many people attempt to save others but do not look after their own needs. If your objective is to always look after others you will starve yourself. Although some of the things I recommend to you may appear simple, there are so few doing it. Although I have spoken much about love, compassion and humbleness, you see so few people with these qualities. Are you compassionate to yourself and others and do you humble yourself before your own God? Many believe that they are God fearing and holy, yet they lack compassion for their fellow brother and sister? Why do people who subscribe to a certain religious ideal try to force others to believe something they themselves do not believe?

I cannot save the human race nor do I need to because the human race does not need to be saved. It needs to grow, to learn and to experience what it is to be God in a human form.

SESSION 16

If you considered what it would be like if the world and all of its inhabitants worked together towards peace and a mutual understanding, you would discover so many new rewards. To assist others not for yourself, but out of kindness, is as much a reward to the helping person as it is to the needy person.

I did not believe that physical illness could be immediately remedied. My philosophy was simply this: if one wanted to remedy his or her physical pains they only needed to ask and I would assist. Of course, most were not equipped to heal themselves and as such, I appeared to be an exceptional healer. To understand how your energy can be exchanged to heal another soul could take years and lifetimes of experience.

It was foreseen before I was born that I would come to earth to heal the multitudes because on a subconscious level people knew I was coming and upon my arrival word spread quickly that there was a messiah. There was much anticipation before I appeared since people had already begun the quest for answers.

Currently, many individuals are beginning their search without the same chaos that occurred during my lifetime as Jesus Christ. There is, however, skepticism and uncertainty about the future and whether peace can exist for everyone and not just a few. Your system has eroded due to confusion, pain and unrelenting corruption as so many seek to become the pillar of success while so few are honest, sincere and compassionate. Those who do believe in goodness are being trampled, disheartened and jaded in their outlook. However, society will not be lost if you can come to realize that you are accountable for not only what you do but also what you do not do.

If you push your brother or sister aside to obtain the chalice of gold, you will discover not only an empty cup but also little reward when you sit alone at the finish with only empty acknowledgements of your achievement. To believe in positions and status is to invest in the idea of a 'fool's gold'. Status has little to do with compassion, love and understanding and if you stood before God, you would not expect Him to accept you because of your status. To create a system that breeds ignorance is to create a perpetual lie that feeds itself. To believe that you are exempt from the ignorance you create is to believe in a punishing God. And if you believe in such a God, that is the world you create for yourself. To remove the barriers of hostility and anger and to tear down the walls of ignorance is to let in your brother and sister and find peace in a world that is unforgiving, relentless, painful and lonely. What you do not see, however, is that the pain, loneliness and barriers are obstacles that you construct because you believe they will protect you. Your own ignorance keeps your perception blurred and has you running in circles.

To travel from lifetime to lifetime without quenching your thirst is like being in a living hell with no end. But to truly understand that hell does not exist requires you to have your thirst quenched and your path lighted to show you the way. In your heart, however, you must first do the work and walk the path, for if you stray from your direction you will realize your hell is only one step away.

SESSION 17

To ponder reincarnation and the possibility that perhaps you have lived on this physical world numerous times before can in itself provide you a sense of self and purpose. However, to truly believe that you have had countless lifetimes may be hard to understand and the thought that you will return again for another lifetime may be too frightening for some. For these ideas, I say facetiously that it would be better then not to look, not to search and not to think. Likewise, society's philosophy is similar; if you do not look, do not search and do not think, there will be little work to do.

To further explain, your development in one lifetime is not based on where you stand in society, how you are measured by your peers, or what physical, emotional, mental or spiritual success you have accomplished. Your development is based purely on your purpose. Inwardly, you are aware of your purpose but nevertheless you do not strive to achieve it because it is easier to follow those around you. Outwardly, you seek answers, people to lead you and for others to do the work you are afraid to do. I am not placing judgement, I just wish to show you that the answers to your life are within.

It is ironic that many look at my existence as Christ and wonder whether I shall appear again as the same soul. What you do not realize is that I appear each time a child is born for within each living soul there is a part of myself as well as a part of yourself. Each entity ultimately comes together as one collective soul, one collective unconscious, to open the doorways for yourself to pass through.

The learning process I speak of only appears to be complicated but when you finally find the path within yourself, all other obstacles will fall away. As you learn to listen to yourself, the pathway will become clearer. You may ask the common question of why you are obsessed with staying youthful and desire to leave your mark in life? The reasons are many. Desiring youth keeps the soul progressing forward and provides it with purpose. Having youth or a sense of it is a desire for the God energy and a part of the collective unconscious which is the unified body of all souls. Also, the desire to stay youthful keeps you working together within the collective unconscious to discover your individual purpose on this earth. Furthermore, the desire for youth encourages thought, creates curiosity and creativity, brings balance and harmony and helps you to pursue a unique expression of your particular lifetime.

If you can conceive of the idea of God, then you can understand your own self-expression in this life. It would be easy for me to say that I have incarnated as some of the great historical figures like Joan of Arc, Henry the VIII, Napoleon, John F. Kennedy, Mother Theresa or Lady Diana, Princess of Wales, but I have not as you also have not. You are who you are and will always remain as your own soul, and when you return to spirit you shall again decide what type of lifetime you will choose and when you shall live. Even if your soul decided to reincarnate and split into five different souls with five different purposes, when each of your souls pass away on the physical plane, they will come back together, to you and to the source known as one collective consciousness called God.

As you learn to understand who and what your desires are, you will learn to take responsibility for your own direction. The next 100 years will force many people and their children to rebel against the 'system', which in reality are the masses forging ahead in a new direction towards a new path. The old ways of thinking are dying off as the evolution of humankind becomes clearer, an evolution that is inevitable on both an individual and social level. Many individuals strongly desire that I return to live amongst them without realizing that I am already here. Likewise, people search so desperately for love but do not see that it is already there. Everybody wants and wants without ever recognizing that even if they fulfilled all of their desires, they would still feel empty.

Some individuals lay bets to beat the odds in order to come out ahead of the rest. They attempt to supercede others only to realize that the bet was lost, even though others may perceive that they have won.

You must understand that the only way to get ahead is to lag behind because whether you lead the pack or sit at the end, you must remain in the same space and the same moment you have created. You must sit with your painful sins, your questions of desire with your lack of perceived love and accomplishments.

At some point, look into the mirror to see your scarred face and soul that has travelled through many lifetimes; only then will you understand that the war you have waged against yourself has been lost, and will you learn to accept defeat and embrace love as your captor. Even though I achieved a great love of self and others, I was still imprisoned by love and its power as I was forced to surrender to my pride over and over again throughout my life. Each time I wanted to stand up and fight, the love from within would softly speak to me and say, "release yourself from this pain". Pride would then appear as my enemy to show that I was strong and invincible. However, upon surrendering, I was released from the physical pain that is so persistent in your reality. I always desired to fight but the expression of my soul was to relent and to give in so as to find peace.

Unlike so many others, I had the gift of self love but did not need others to laud my abilities as others require. Only when you discover that love is in itself an entity of its own will you understand its true meaning and expression. You are led to believe that God only creates love between two souls who are worthy. However, it is up to you to create love if you choose and desire it.

It may take ten years or a lifetime to find either God or love. Each remains only a short time and then quickly flees, not because you are undeserving but because you must learn to conquer your pride and understand that neither love nor God can be conquered or called upon to do your bidding. You are here to sacrifice yourself to your own higher self, and then find harmony and love between the two masters, the physical God that bids to you outwardly and the physical God that bids to you internally. To understand that both of these elements make up your world is what will give you the momentum to move forward.

SESSION 18

One way to unlock your subconscious and discover the truth about your soul and all of your lifetimes is through the Akashic[5] records. But before you access this information, it is prudent to be aware that you must accept great responsibility for it. You may desire to access this information to further understand your purpose or to uncover information which may encourage you to grow, to understand and to develop. To access the Akashic records simply say:

> Within my soul, destiny and fate are connected.

> Within my vision is the sight of past, present and future events.

> With wisdom and knowledge, I access for my higher self and the souls that guide me information and understanding of all that is.

> I create within myself protection, knowing, understanding and God's love to allow me to access this information.

> May it always lead me to greater understanding of myself, those who guide me and the many souls who are with me on this physical plane.

One does not need to repeat this expression time and time again. You need only say it once and your pathway and development will begin to unfold. But as I have said, be aware that once the door is opened, there is no turning back. So upon making the decision to access this information you will no longer be able to shut your soul off from it. If you are looking for a higher purpose and a greater understanding of life, this is one avenue to access this knowledge. Be prepared for great changes, some difficult but each rewarding inwardly and outwardly nonetheless. In delivering these words to you now, understand that you

---

5 The Akashic Records is said to be a library within the metaphysical realm which contains all information, past, present and future, about each soul, their different lifetimes and purposes, as well as information about the universe and its existence.

have made the choice to draw in a greater understanding of yourself and your purpose.

During my time as Jesus Christ, most souls were much more unfortunate than myself, spiritually, emotionally, financially and so on. Currently, however, you are even less fortunate in other ways as you frantically search just as people in my time also searched. If you do not grab the opportunity and discover what it is you are looking for, will it be years, lifetimes or an eternity before the opportunity will come again? The question is in the answer just as the answer is in the question. To observe the sky above at night is to observe a reflection of God in its finest form. If you look upon the millions and millions of brightly lit stars, you as an individual are a star shining brightly in a truly dark world. The darkness, however, is a necessary evil if one wishes to see the stars shine. During the day only the sun itself is shining and the stars remain hidden from view, and like the stars during daylight, there are many times in your life when you believe you are also hidden from view. Allow yourself to know that even though your appearance is obscured in daylight, inevitably it will become dark again and your star will be seen shining brighter than ever before. You will have an opportunity to shine brightly whether in this lifetime or another, and you shall have the opportunity to stand out. Be patient with your progress, be at peace with your star, and don't covet the sun's light for as it comes, it too must pass.

If you decide to create what you think may be a more rewarding life, do not look to others for love, support or to have others follow you. Do whatever is necessary for yourself and allow others to make their own decisions. If I had wanted you to follow me, think like me and be like me, would you still be unique? You can hear, understand and even love me, and that in itself can help you to change and impact others simply by example.

I speak to those who wish to listen for they enjoy the melodies that my soul creates. You shall create different songs but certainly no less important than mine.

SESSION 19

Many individuals questioned my purpose and believed I existed to lead and shed light on the earth's many inhabitants. But while my purpose was to show people love and compassion, I was neither selfish nor did I desire popularity, wealth or status. As unusual as it may sound, my purpose was destined long before my arrival. I was aware in spirit of the ramifications of coming to your world as the soul of Jesus Christ, just as you are aware of your circumstances before you arrive. However, when you live in the physical world, circumstances change, difficulties are encountered, obstacles arise and your destiny and fate appear uncertain. Pursuing my purpose was not an easy choice but as I grew and learned and acknowledged within myself what I had come to achieve, many of my problems fell away.

You may believe that your circumstances are different or less important, but I see little difference when compared to mine. I am aware that you like to think of yourself as insignificant when you are not. You may assume that the purpose of any great leader has greater importance but a leader is often provided with more attributes and skills to more easily deal with the objective they have undertaken. You, however, have just as much to cope with if you have less assets at your disposal. I never believed nor endorsed the theory of leadership which is the reason why I accepted all who came into my path. Many wanted me to lead but I did not choose it. The role was thrust upon me although it was difficult for me to accept. I encouraged others to follow their own path, to understand their own needs and to believe in themselves.

History can be cruel in many ways as reflected in the many religious teachings that have looked upon me as the saviour to whom people pray to forgive crimes and sins that most have never even committed. How can I absolve you from something you have not done? How can I be your God when you are already God? How can I sacrifice my life when you have already sacrificed yours? How can I be pure and innocent and still live and breathe the same air as you? And if you are human and taught that I have not faltered, how can you possibly follow in my footsteps if I am someone who is supposed to be out of reach? I emphasize the point, I am not your God and never will be. No matter what you are taught or decide to believe, you will eventually understand that you are your own person, your own God and your own devil—three in one.

When you look to your past and attempt to draw truth from something that does not exist, you will begin to see that you must rely on your own capabilities and thoughts. Furthermore, as you usher in a new era and start to envision that which will unfold, you will begin to see that my words are true.

From the time you were young, you were taught right from wrong, as well as about other countries, their cultures and their differences. However, you were not taught to see how people are similar and as a result, you fail to see how you are similar to me. Since I was also human I could also feel, think, breathe, eat and drink, so why would you look upon other cultures differently when you realize they require the same elements as you to survive? My purpose as Christ was to teach, but a teacher is only as good as his or her pupils; if I had no one to teach, I too would have no purpose. And now, as I speak through this soul, Dale Landry, again I have purpose but this time as a teacher, not as a leader. In being a teacher, I have had to learn to humble myself and I have respected and understood what I could not change. To be a leader requires ignorance and leadership which is self defined and created through one's own desires and needs. Thus, if you forego the opportunity to lead yourself to your objectives, then your life purpose will seem unjustified.

Even in death, my heart still craved the love that I was unable to embrace in my life. With this idea, I may not be a lesser or weaker person for not having obtained love's company, but was I a fool for not having done so? When I return once again will the waters of love rush over me like the moon's light floods the earth?

Do each of you believe our purposes are that similar? Do you believe it is possible to be tainted by physical love? Can we relieve ourselves of conscious thought so that we don't have to look for our soul's destiny?   If we are harmonious as a society will the universe fulfil our collective objective? Do you doubt eternal life? Do you not understand that what you crave within and hide outwardly is secretly what your brother and sister also desire? Is it so difficult to imagine that my desires are the same as yours? Must we listen to words we do not believe and accept that we cannot have what we desire simply because we are told we cannot have it?

If you decide to pursue your path and use hope as your companion, shall you find peace if you first do not sacrifice love? If you cannot humble yourself, do you believe you shall never be humbled? When you knock on death's door and come face-to-face with yourself, will you smile and say that you have sacrificed much for love and are pleased with the outcome, or will you feel empty after having passed through the door of life with merely the wind brushing your face with little, if any, touch to the heart?

I wonder if you truly hear these words I speak that come from the sight I have been given and the past that I know. I am aware that many will follow but few will hear them. To this soul, Dale Landry, who has provided his time to me, I will remain close by him until he shall pass into spirit, not because I owe him a debt, but because the enemy he will face is one that I have faced and I shall show him the way through the obstacles that I was unable to pass through. So my voice shall remain as one with his, not to colour his future or obstruct his path, but to shed light where it is needed.

As you seek rest on your journey, stop for a moment and listen to the wind, and if there is no wind, look to the sun; and if the sun is blocked by the clouds, then listen to your heart; and if your heart is pained, then call out to your soul. If your soul does not reply, you will know you are dead.

SESSION 20

History has shown that the same mistakes are continually repeated, just as we remain uncertain as to why we step into the same problems only to ignite the situation once again. Most of the world's worst afflictions have been created through wars. Unfortunately, the countless souls which have died from war are quickly forgotten.

During my life there was constant conflict supported by the belief that war was required to resolve it. Sadly enough, however, in the coming years war will rear its ugly head once more and everyone will be the loser as pain will be ever present in each soul that is forced to watch a sister, brother, mother, father, neighbour or friend needlessly die. There is little I can do to intervene when the decision is made to go to war. The one that casts the first stone believes that his hands are tied and as a consequence all others believe that they can do little to stop the slaughter.

Now my question to you is this: When your war has been fought and your economies begin to rebuild themselves was the pride of ignorance worth the loss of loved ones? To some the answer is 'yes', and those in power may answer that war is 'for the good of all human kind'. If as Christ I took the role as a leader, would I speak alone or would I speak for all who followed? If I was to lead, apparently I would be speaking on my own for those who were following would believe that I knew what I was doing. So take heed of the words that I am saying and my question now is if someone strikes a blow, do you retaliate or turn the other cheek? I believe you should wait to see whether the blow was struck before the individual realized he or she made a hasty decision. Many wars developed from the assumption that an opposing country would strike first when in fact they intended to remain docile.

I would urge you to be patient in these trying times that lay before you as tempers will be short and emotions will ride high. I fear less for adults who are capable of choosing their own direction but it is the senseless killing of children and the parents who rear them that I mourn. To those who needlessly have blood on their hands, may your soul discover forgiveness in your motives for pursuing war.

SESSION 21

The main focus of the 21st century will be to rebuild society as new languages will be created and people will discover the importance of their past. Archeological digs will unearth many new bones and villages, and much of history before my lifetime as Christ will be rewritten. Ancient scrolls and manuals will also be discovered that will disclose many unknown languages that existed before my time.

Skeptics will always doubt the information but it will be up to each individual to determine whether the information is accurate. Within each soul is a record of the countless lifetimes lived as well as a record of all the people and places visited and experienced in each lifetime. In the 21st century, it will become commonplace to desire to learn your past and seek more information about yourself. Many theoretical books concerning humankind will be written to educate people of what history itself has missed. I provide you with this information concerning the past and future only to help you in this moment to understand your purpose.

My lifetime as Jesus Christ has played a significant role in shaping history as you understand it but in the future much will be discovered to reshape history once again. The information written about me however is circumstantial and it is your privilege to believe only what you desire. If you allow your heart to feel, you will intuitively know what is true and what is false. Only until one can learn to speak in tongues as I did can one understand the language that I spoke, and only then can one understand how God, the angels and spirit work, as well as the love each feels for each other. I spoke in riddles not so much because it was how I was taught but because it was how God and spirit spoke to me. In each riddle is a deeper meaning and an understanding that goes far beyond the words themselves. However, God will not punish you for not knowing the meaning of my message since it is more important to know that you do not need pain and sickness in learning compassion and humbleness. Only when you truly believe this will you understand that the afflictions you have brought upon yourself are not required to shape your future, your present or even your past.

You may believe that the fear of fire and brimstone will keep you from sinning when in reality it only leads you to a self-created hell since it presupposes that you believe in a God that is unjust and unloving? If you believe this, your reality will be based in fear and not love. Furthermore, if a child is created out of love but rejected with scorn and distaste throughout its life, did God reject the child or the pain of the parents who created it?

Although you are obsessed with the absence of love, sincerity and honesty in this world, you perpetuate the same ignorance through your own way of living. If you are incapable of changing yourself, how can you possibly change the world you live in. If you cannot see life in a better light, how can others? Hope is not something that humankind has created, it is an aspect of love that should be ever present in your life. If you expect to achieve without challenge, accordingly I must ask whether you give as easily as you expect to receive?

Money rules the world's economies. It has grown substantially since my life but the same greed and desire continues. Money is neither good nor evil yet it holds an incredible power over people's words and actions. Money, although it does not have soul, can change a person's purpose. Money cannot love but it can stop one from loving. If money is all that you seek, where is your God? If you live by the sword, you will die by the sword, and if you live for money you will end up dying without it, but with the wish of having it.

If your neighbour is incapable of feeding and clothing his or her young, do you believe it is just hard luck or are you willing to give up a piece of yourself and make their luck better? Do you fashion yourself after those who are beautiful, or do you love someone for what lies below the surface? Do you accept someone because they are of importance or are well-known, or do you attract to those who will inspire and support you in your endeavours just as you support theirs?

If you see your world as troubled and with little hope, would you take refuge in a negative attitude as others do or would you create some joy in a world that seems empty? These words may ring as an echo from your past or perhaps they are words your parents used to say or an idea your soul has always carried. Your children cannot understand the true values of life if you offer them only the greedy and superficial goals you have aspired to. If I as Jesus Christ have played such an important role in your teachings, why do my values of compassion, humbleness and desire for everyone's best interest seem so unimportant? If you truly believe in your religious temple, why do you still lack love, empathy and honesty? Why do you fear and allow damnation to play such an important role in your world? Why do you want to punish and ostracize those who do not believe what you do about God? Is it not hate that initiates your wars? Is hate an emotion I taught? Many have used both my name and God's to wage battle, yet no one will ever go to war with my blessing.

May God uncover your ears and eyes to allow you to hear and see. May He still your tongue to allow you to speak. And may your heart find its path and know death so that your soul can rejoice in the pain of knowing that it has discovered love.

SESSION 22

When I lived, there was a story I often told to those who gathered to listen. It was about a young boy named David who spent most of his time playing alone but at times he worked closely with his father. One day David's father passed away, and because he did not understand death he was confused and pained, and no longer wanted to play or do the things he used to. As this young boy grew older, he approached life with a serious attitude. There was little laughter and no desire for love because inwardly he felt that he had also died with his father. David had no explanation for his feelings and did not feel the same desires as other young people his age. But one day, David met a new friend, another young man, and they immediately became kindred spirits. They came together often, never tiring of one another's company. Soon David realized that once again his heart felt light and there was love for his companion.

Initially, the thought of loving someone so strongly frightened him, however the idea of letting him go was too much to bear. So together as friends they grew into manhood and David's friend soon found a wife and settled down. While the nature of their friendship had changed due to the marriage, there was still a strong connection of love. However, instead of marrying, David decided to travel to foreign lands which for to him was a marriage of sorts, a life journey unlike what others would commit to. He travelled for many years and met many strange and wonderful people. David found the experience often difficult and lonely but at other times experienced great compassion and love.

Years later, David decided to return home and upon his arrival his old friend was there to greet him. They embraced and spoke as if they had never parted. His friend asked about his travels and David explained all that he had seen and the riches of his experience. In return, David asked his friend about his journey. "I have seen much," said David's friend, "because in all the places you have travelled, all the people you have met, all the love that you have felt, you shared these things with me in my heart and now I am rewarded from your experience."

David remained quiet listening to his friend and then said, "My reward was knowing that you were always there with me and your communication of love kept me safe. And now that I have returned home, I am aware of your experience of love."

The following day, David passed away; the only people who came to his burial were his friend and his son. The son asked his father, "Who was this man? Was he your friend?" The father replied, "He was to me what the moon is to the stars, what the wind is to the earth, and what the water is to a sailboat." "What do you mean?" the son asked. The father looked at his son as the tears rolled from his eyes and said, "I could never tell you how much you mean to me. My love for you is so strong that it is difficult for me to put into words the breath of life that this friend has given to me. But whether he is here with me or not, like yourself, he will always be the wind in my sails that carries me through the troubled waters into the night's setting sun."

You often try to define and understand love, but in your experience love is limited in a way so that your heart only feels gratified and enriched. What you do not recognize is that love touches those who are open to it in no matter what form it may grace in their life. Your world believes that love can only occur between two people who make a commitment or a vow of marriage but what about love between two, three, four or more individuals who share a similar experience? You should not seek a short-term encounter that will provide you only a brief scent of a radiant garden but you should search for a garden in which you can plant your own seeds, harvest your own foods and germinate your own flowers to blossom.

When you look at other people, do not ask if they will treat you fairly or kindly but simply feel blessed that they have arrived to share their thoughts with you in whatever capacity they do so. If you can trust in all that exists and in all that love can conjure up, then you can be certain that the trust and love you so strongly desire will be reciprocated by this other individual through a mutual understanding of life. To expect others to be there for you is to expect yourself to give to someone what you cannot, because what you ask of others is what you believe you lack in yourself. For instance, if you ask your partner if they love you, you obviously have no love for yourself. But if you can accept all that your partner provides, with no questions and demands, in due time, he or she shall say "I love you", because they will already see that you have it within yourself.

To communicate in love is to humble yourself. To believe you are fragile, human and unexceptional is to recognize your beauty and foster your feelings of love which cannot be expressed in words. You love the sparrow that flies freely as well as the injured bird you must care for; when you are broken, you can still be loved just as can one who flies freely and travel to places with the heart that others cannot. To truly soar in love, your heart must be crushed in order to understand the voice of love that speaks so softly.

If you have a sound mind and are physically strong with few weaknesses of the heart, love may not permeate your soul because you simply do not require it. I am not saying that you should make yourself weak in order to have love, but do not cage your heart so others cannot get in and you cannot get out.

In my travels as Jesus Christ, I met a young woman who had asked me for directions and in my own foolish pride I felt wiser for being able to guide her. Once she received the information, she unexpectedly asked if I knew where I was going. Surprised by her question, I stopped for a moment, looked deep into her eyes and began to feel ashamed because I realized that this young woman had come to offer me directions and a warning. And the reason I felt foolish was because I came to understand that those individuals who I had perceived as weak were not less fortunate, but were just as wise if not wiser than myself. I learned humility from this experience as well as the ability to listen to what others are truly asking me.

On another occasion a friend invited me to dinner and I graciously accepted. The evening progressed well and everyone enjoyed themselves considerably. At one point after dinner a young man close to my own age approached me and asked me to spend some time with him. I accepted and we went off to the garden to talk. He asked my thoughts on love, friendship and life and in no time we were very involved in a conversation about what was important to him as well as my experiences. Towards the end of the evening we were still alone talking and the last question he asked was if I would ever experience love? Once again, much like the young woman who I had given directions to, I felt a sharp pain in my heart as I understood to whom I was speaking. To give myself time, I asked him what he meant and in the next moment the young man disappeared. By this time, however, the dinner had ended and everybody had dispersed and I was still sitting alone in the garden. So I sat there for the rest of the night pondering this man's question to me about love. Although I thought I had experienced love when the question was asked I knew well that love had not yet graced my door. I felt that I could not cry for the pain was too deep to express, so I just sat alone, in my thoughts, and when the morning sun arose, I was still sitting there unable to move or even to hear my own breath.

What challenge had this fellow friend bestowed upon me when I considered myself to be so wise, yet was truly inexperienced. To what did I owe the absence of love in my heart and the emptiness of my soul? Finally, I left the garden and wandered the village streets, seeing only blank faces pass me by. After two days, I met a stranger in a dark robe who asked, "Where are you going good sir?" My reply was quick without thought, "I do not know." In that moment I understood the essence of love; love was the experience of not knowing where I was going or who I was. And when I looked up to see the man in the black robe, he too had vanished and again I realized to whom I had spoken.

When I arrived back to my place of rest, I took solace once more in the garden and sat alone to gaze at the moon. The Archangel Michael appeared next to me exuding the most radiant and beautiful colours.

"Of what do you think?," Michael asked.

"I think of nothing," I replied.

"Of what do you feel?," he said.

"I feel nothing," I replied once more.

"Of what do you desire?," Michael continued.

"I desire nothing."

"Who are you?," Michael asked further.

"I am nothing," I responded.

"Then for what do you live?," he stated.

I sat for a long time and thought about the question, "I do not know for what I live."

"So why do you live,?" Michael continued on.

I said, "I live because my heart beckons me forward and my soul cries out to go home."

"And where is home and to what does your heart beckon?"

I replied, "My heart beckons me to a language I cannot speak, the language of love, and my soul cries to go home which is where my heart resides."

"And what shall you do?," Michael asked once more.

"I do not know."

Michael took his right hand, placed it under my chin, lifted my face and peered deeply into my eyes. He went on, "What you seek is what you shall find; what you find, you already have; what you already have, you do not know; and when you find what you do not have, you will know and shall have peace. When your heart dies and your soul cries out no longer then you are at one with the rest of your family at their place in the universe. At this moment you will discover that life is a puzzle to complete and your journey a path to finish. There will be no need to long for, to cry or feel pain. If you know the words I speak within your heart and your soul, you will understand the language of love and your journey is finished."

With this final statement he was gone and henceforth I no longer understood my purpose, who I was or what I wanted. I had been stripped of all worldly possessions and my heart and soul were left naked for all to see. From these experiences I offer the following message:

> We must each bare our heart and soul in order to understand our journey, our purpose and our desires, and come home to the master that lies within each of us, to release ourselves from that which we think is truth but is not.

SESSION 23

There is a lot about my past you will probably never know just as there is a lot about your own past you will also never know. If you decide to compare yourself to others, their approach to life, what they have achieved, their past, their family and their friends, you will discover incredible similarities. When you look at your parents, you will see astounding similarities, some comfortable and others not. It was assumed that I had no problems accepting my parents, friends and associates. I treated everyone equally and this was an easy task.

From an early age, I knew that both of my parents served as doorways into uncharted waters. They were the answers and the questions to my being, and on some intellectual level my mother and my father knew the difficulties I would experience in choosing my life as Jesus Christ. Although I was similar to both of them, I was also my own person, an individual. There were characteristics from each that I chose to keep and others I left behind, just as there were elements I chose from my personal environment and others from my past lives. You may question why you are so much like your parents but do you ever question the path you have chosen in your life, for example, who you are, where you came from and what aspect of God you are? If you mapped out your own individual path, your present life as well as your past incarnations, you would understand the road you are taking now.

The singularity of your direction and its inevitable outcome is not about taking up a challenge in life, about conquering the hands of time or about beckoning love, and it is certainly not about suffering or about conquering. Life goes beyond words, it goes beyond the description that you can give to God. It goes beyond heaven, hell or purgatory. Life is something that leaves you with a sense of unexpressed emotions and thoughts. To give you an easy answer would be like removing you from your life. To remove you from your life is not a simple task.

Life is like a butterfly, the metamorphosis of a caterpillar to a cocoon to a beautifully winged insect. And, when you outgrow the cocoon, the wings you sprout only come in death, not life. So there are two sides to life and death as you know it and do not understand it; each world is totally different. I am sure that a caterpillar has no comprehension of what it would be like to fly, yet through its metamorphosis and period of death, its being comes to understand its potential to fly and leaves behind the past to take on flight and new purpose in the skies above. Yet, the butterfly's seemingly momentary life span is much like a human's in that in the blink of an eye it is gone. What can possibly be accomplished from this constant repetition of life and then death? That is the question. How many times must you evolve before you can understand why you would do the same thing over and over again?

If everything in life has its purpose, what is the purpose of humankind? What place do you have in being here? The answer is both simple and obvious, yet unrecognized. You live life because it is an expression of who you are. Clearly, this is hard to conceive because until you can move beyond the obstacles you have created, until you can see beyond your fears, and until you can shift from your conscious mind to your subconscious, you will not understand your insignificance in an unimportant world that drifts aimlessly through space and time yet is still destined wherever it may go. But even though your world has no importance, there is still completeness, purpose and significance. To have one, you must have the other. For instance, to be beautiful, you must be ugly; to have faith, you must disbelieve; to cry, you must laugh; and, to be popular, you must live in painful solitude.

There are many ways to explain the world around you and many ways to see what isn't before your eyes. Through death I found the doorway to life and as you take heed of the words I speak, you shall find power within the essence of who you are. What I speak isn't anything you have not heard before or what you did not already know in your own heart. It may appear that you only live in this life but there is not one living person now who did not exist when I existed as Jesus Christ. Just as the world's population has grown since that time in history, your soul in the metaphysical dimension has split and multiplied ten fold. This however has not taken away from what you experienced at the time we were together. So, from lifetime to lifetime, you exist in some way, shape or form and when a powerful soul, such as Indira Ghandi or Mother Theresa reincarnates, that soul returns carrying with it all of the information it has learned from its previous lifetimes.

I have explained many things in so many different ways that they may appear confusing and indecipherable, however, when you hear the truth, you will recognize it. The difficulty is that you do not always hear the complete truth, so you only recognize your life as part of the picture. Through the soul's incarnation, at one time in history, you too were a greatly renowned soul. However, you should not thrive for greatness but thrive for growth and purpose. You now exist in a time when a great breakthrough will occur. It is a period where you will come to understand much and see opportunity in ways you have not seen in the past. You are coming into a time when you will be moving back towards the light and as a result information will be available much more easily, your thoughts will be much sharper and your physical energy can be produced and manufactured within the physical body at greater speeds. You will come to understand your journey, your purpose and how to experience the most from your existence. This will not remove your fears for existing, your limitations to personal growth, or your perpetual ignorance but you will understand that your differences serve to propel you forward to accomplish what you could not before.

If I told you that you were a popular soul in your past life like Catherine the Great, Julius Caesar or Florence Nightingale would you accept your greatness or believe this to be impossible? I say that whatever appears impossible is very likely to have happened because without one you cannot have the other. If you recognize and accept the possibility of your past greatness, how will you feel knowing that at one time you had achieved so much? If you knew beyond a shadow of doubt that you had a life as a popular figure would you want to preach the word of God or would it propel you into searching for higher goals and purpose and force you to be kinder to others? Would it impact you to uncover your inner most desires? If you walked in my shoes and spoke in my voice, how would you think differently, what would you challenge and who would you seek out in life to speak with? Would you deny your greatness, would you accept your ignorance, would you allow your ugliness to suppress you and would you still believe that your ignorance would stop you from achieving? Does your perspective change in knowing, understanding, believing or thinking that you once walked in my shoes? And what shatters the glass of illusion once you take my hand? Why do you believe that you are weak and incapable of achieving anything. What is in the essence of my words that allows you to believe you can achieve anything you desire and what do you now understand that you did not understand before? In knowing that you once had a life as something more divine then you are now, why are you suddenly elevated from nobody to somebody and why is it unimportant whether others recognize you? Do you see the importance in just living your own life, regardless of how others view you?

I can tell you the answer to these questions. Whether you were great or popular in a past life is irrelevant. In each physical life you existed, you denied yourself your greatness which makes it difficult for you now to believe that you were great. Take my hand and hold it tightly. Know that you are loved and work hard to understand it, and soon you will no longer need to rely on these words.

SESSION 24

From the shadows of life comes an understanding of where the soul is searching to find rest. It is never in the busiest times of your life that you experience the most of the moment but rather when you spend quiet time alone. In the confusion and turmoil of your everyday living, you cannot fully concentrate on your own thoughts because there is so much interaction with so many other souls aspiring to find the same thing you are searching for which is contentment. You may assume that material possessions and higher education will provide you inner contentment but this is not the case. It is a matter of listening to your soul to discover your inner happiness. What the human soul fails to recognize is that the conscious and subconscious minds are one and the same and when you are conscious you do know what the soul is saying but when you are asleep you do not recognize the images your soul is describing. The soul is aware on a certain intellectual level that if you listen to your conscious and subconscious minds, you will be cognizant of what it is telling you.

The soul speaks directly to your conscious and subconscious minds and the messages can be clear. However, the confusion of everyday life can easily obstruct the messages that are coming through. For instance, the soul may impress upon your conscious mind to be still, but the conscious mind may in turn reply "I can't be, there are problems that I need to address. If I don't worry about them, something could go wrong. I need to constantly be alert." So, in your dream state your soul may say to your subconscious "Do not be afraid of what is coming." Your dream may involve a great deal of darkness and turmoil and upon awakening you may feel very afraid and believe that the darkness represents a terrible situation. This may cause your conscious mind to worry instead of recognizing that your soul is speaking to you in images that the conscious mind does not clearly recognize. Your conscious mind is directed through your subconscious, so if your conscious is not aware of how the subconscious works, then you will have difficulties communicating with your soul. To understand your soul, you must understand the images, thoughts and the knowingness that it speaks.

Your soul may say to your conscious mind, "You are not in love."

But your conscious mind will believe, "Oh, but I am. I have to be. No one else has loved me and this person is very special."

The soul may then wait patiently and after a short while may say, "This relationship is going to cause you great difficulties. Let it go."

But your conscious mind will believe, "I can't. I'm ugly. I'm unwanted and unloved, and this is my last opportunity for happiness."

As a final effort your soul will say, "Know your path and retreat until your conscious mind has learned through the pain of your heart that the long journey was unnecessary and that the pain of your journey was not needed."

Your soul will often communicate not to the heart but to your conscious mind. But if the heart is listening, it will say, "Yes, these words are true. It is best to follow."

If the heart is confused and upset, however, your conscious mind in its wisdom may reply, "We need to wait for the heart until it has rested and is at peace before we make our decision."

And only after the heart is resting will it reply once again, "I am uncertain of what the soul speaks but I believe it is best to follow whatever it is saying."

If you cast your nets into the waters of your subconscious you will obtain much food of thought to feast on because in your subconscious there are many different thoughts that you may not know exist within yourself. To harvest your subconscious is to bring the light of day to the darkness of your soul. It is giving the soul a chance to breathe, to know it is being listened to and that its purpose is being accomplished. To waste away lifetime after lifetime is neither wrong nor right for eventually the soul finds its purpose in the conscious mind and obtains great peace in doing so. It is not for you to judge whether you are capable of understanding your soul since this is a difficult task. Your role and purpose is to listen to what your soul says and to follow it, no matter how painful the road ahead may seem. And upon doing so, you will understand the same thing I had discovered which is that there is rest amidst the storm. There is peace and tranquility in confusion, love in the desert, release from prison, and love and acceptance in shame, all while living in this physical world.

You may ask what the purpose is in listening to your soul when you must live in such a painful world and why you must travel from one life to another with no end in sight. My reply is simple; when you know the language that your soul speaks, you can show your neighbour and friend by example what you have found since it is through human instinct that you desire to compete for and kill for what those around you have. Once you discover inner peace collectively, you will learn to speak a universal language you do not yet know; one that will guide you towards an understanding that does not yet exist but has in past. As I have mentioned already, when you are linked as one your true purpose will then be understood. When you know why you are here and are linked to your soul and the information that is held therein, you can start to make changes to your physical life that were never possible before.

In my time as Jesus Christ, I spoke of this universal language. I tried to help the elders also understand it but they did not want to hear. So I was turned away to the masses who were perhaps more ignorant but still willing to listen. Even though the ignorant did not understand much of what I spoke of, they understood what I said on a soul level and retained the information, just like an incarnation in that time period, you are clearly still aware. This language of knowing can be referred to as God's Language, a language of peace spoken in love. When you are angry and strike out, do you listen to your heart or does the heart not listen to the mind's direction to the soul? If you were capable of forgiving all those who angered you in this lifetime, would you forgive them? Would you truly trust your heart to let go of the burden it carries and are you capable of letting go of past injustices? The answer must be 'yes'. So what stops you from forgiving and what stops the heart and the conscious mind from lifting the weight of your anger and needless thoughts? Do you resent the many lifetimes you had yet do not understand? What will it take for you to give up your resentment? Do you hope that with time an opportunity will come around to have revenge on God's injustice and will you have the opportunity to hurt others who did not love you when they should have?

If you come to a quiet place where you realize that all of your anger and resentment mean nothing but wastefully occupy storage space that you need for love and peace, would you take action to let it go? What will it take for you to pull up anchor, raise your sails and head out to sea to make that journey once again? If you harbor resentment, do you stay fixed in one place and lose sight of the world and the many things it has to offer? Your soul is much the same as an ocean in that it can carry you to many unchartered lands and seas and show you things you never knew existed before.

When you stop making excuses and discover that love can conquer anger and pain, you can then use the love in your heart to shield you in times of misfortune, and turn to the quietness of your soul that speaks so many different languages. It is through the soul and the language it speaks that the doors to what you search for will open and you shall pass through easily regardless of the obstacles that stand in your way. On a subconscious level, you will always understand others through knowing your heart and soul because all people speak the same language. You are living in this physical world for one purpose and soon you will know what it is; from there, you shall have peace.

SESSION 25

As Christ, I had friends, acquaintances and people in high places who tried to persuade me to take on the role of leader and to show the people the direction towards finding themselves. In showing them their path I would often ask, "What is it within you that you desire so strongly to go to war." They would look confused by my question and not really understand what I had asked. I explained to those with confused expressions how war is an inevitable result. If you have a group of people lead by one person, there is only one thinker to lead the flock. So if there is a contention within the group and the leader responds in a manner only few of the people desire, he is no longer considered fit and must be removed from his post. This can lead to greater dissension and ultimately war to justify the demands of a limited few. The demands, however, may not occur as you expect. They may be as simple as conquering others to show they are feeble and weak. For this reason, I did not desire the role of leader and as a result death was my punishment since it was believed I had betrayed those who only desired that I lead them. In time, if people come to understand that through one collective consciousness everyone can be heard, then they will realize that there is no longer a need for war. If all of the world's people, their resources and efforts were used to support, love and erase the world's sickness and pain, it would take only forty to fifty years of a concentrated effort to overcome many of the globe's current problems. Sadly, however, it is 2,000 years since I have lived and little movement has taken place to solve the many problems.

When you understand that the wars around the globe are an expression of your own inner turmoil you will understand the reason for why they occur. But if you do not forgive yourself for your own inner battle, you certainly cannot forgive others for the wars on your planet. To deny that you can change your inner struggle is to also believe that you cannot. To expect that change must take a long time to evolve, is like assuming that you have never been here before and that too is an assumption.

People feel a sense of safety in categorizing others into classes and groups. For instance, you may feel safe in being called a wife or someone's mother. However, safety for women is sometimes expressed to the extent that they are possessed by a man. And for a man, safety and satisfaction is achieved when they are accepted by their peers based on their material accolades. People are content to be placed in a box and wish to be absolved of the responsibility of stepping outside it. But if you are not accepted and feel unsafe, do you turn away from the fold and ignore the status quo or do you allow yourself to be a scapegoat for your family's losses or shame? Do you own your dignity and respect or do you believe that these characteristics must be acquired from others?

There are so many bright and beautiful hues within the earth's prism. Unfortunately most only see the most visible ones, but those who are gifted will notice at least 2,000 colours in the rainbow. I often question why the world's gifted people are viewed so strangely while those who are less gifted are perceived as worthwhile providers for the future? Why do people spend so little time to think, analyze, perceive, understand and offer compassion to life and the things around them? If I lived in your world today, would I wear clothes that would conform to your standards? Would my teeth be straight and white, would I live in a certain area and would I have the right friends? Would I appear to be politically correct enough to achieve popularity and would I be able to cross all boundaries and be understood by the multitudes? Have things become better since the time I lived or have people regressed? If your brother, sister, friend, neighbour or stranger does not dress or speak your language, then how could I achieve such expectations in your world?

If you believe that I am there for you, why would I not be there equally for someone else? If I accept the poor, can I also accept the rich and if I encourage the ignorant, can I also love those who are blind? If I am lost in your city, can I find my way through the forest? If I cannot walk, will you carry me? If I am ashamed, can you forgive me? If I do not please you, am I still accepted?

You falter not in what you cannot accept or love but in your misunderstanding that all people you come into contact with will reflect your fears, thoughts and beliefs about who you are, something you will truly understand only in death. What you hate and dislike in others is what you hate and dislike in yourself. You live in a world of illusion because no matter who you look at, they will reflect back some aspect of yourself, from this lifetime or another, and how others view you is dependent upon your current emotional state.

So many people followed and listened to me because they saw an aspect of themselves when they gazed upon me which was the light known as God and the oneness and understanding of their own beauty and perception. But in my death—not the literal death as you perceive it—they saw the darker side of myself, the side that could not forgive myself for being human. When I could not rise above this imperfection, I too was destroyed out of fear, resentment and ignorance, however, those who destroyed me were only damaging the part of themselves that they could have loved. In spirit, we live on to conquer the reality viewed as mortality and immortality, and to embrace a oneness with life and death.

To comprehend your life objective is a difficult feat since you only believe that you must travel on a pathway of God, of goodness, of peace, of serenity, of honesty and of compassion. You may have only started on your pathway towards God where others may take many more lifetimes to achieve the end result. It is important not to see yourself as holy or above your brother and sister because if you see yourself as superior to others, you are truly ignorant and it will become far more difficult for you to learn humility. The religious dogma you have learned places God in a box, so if you decide to love and follow Him, you too must fit into the same box that you have created. You must eliminate these outdated beliefs and find alternate ways of understanding yourself and what God truly means to you.

To fear God and His power is to fear the rules that have been passed down through the centuries. History has shown how many individuals were killed for their beliefs around God while others were punished for not following His word. Now more than ever modern society says you can believe what you want but you still hold strong to the subconscious belief that you will be punished for not following the Lord's ideals and teachings.

If you wish to encounter God in your dream state, how do you think He would come to you? Would He be gentle and kind, loving and beautiful, harmonious and sensitive, insightful and clear, or would He come with fire and brimstone, hate and anger, damnation and punishment? God encompasses all that exists but He does not judge. While you may sense fear and punishment, God neither condones nor condemns these emotions. You choose your perception as a part of your path just as you choose your desires. Understand that the idea I present to you about God is the greatest challenge you will ever encounter because how you understand God is how you will understand yourself.

SESSION 26

When I spoke to the multitudes, I often used parables to give clearer messages and help people more easily understand the lessons to be learned. There was one parable in particular about a man with two sons who was very rich, but also kind and just. One day, one of his sons came to him and asked for his inheritance so he could go out and seek his fortune. The wise father agreed to his son's request and provided the son a good portion of his inheritance. Some time later, the son returned with no money and a down trodden heart. The father then asked the son what he had learned on his journey. The son simply replied that God had taught him well.

In this experience, the father and son rejoiced and the son remained at home to work for his father and build a responsible life where he could enjoy the fruits of his labour. His second son asked his father why he gave the first son his inheritance only to squander it and then accept him back so readily. The father explained that the first son had followed his heart and did what he felt was best even if it seemed wrong to others. The father further explained that if one is not allowed to make mistakes then one is not allowed to learn. At the end of the conversation, the father finally said, "You have stayed with me and have done well as a result, but you remained for security and your objective was to be rewarded for your efforts. In doing so, you limited your potential and capabilities, and have therefore limited your opportunity and thinking because if you follow in my footsteps, you do not walk to the beat of your own heart." To this the son was initially puzzled, angry and upset but over time he understood his father's words and eventually he left home with no inheritance and without a direction. Upon his return the second son was healthy, wealthy and wise from his own insightful discoveries.

It is difficult to comprehend life's many challenges but if you listen and question your faults, your short comings and your assets, you can accept who and what you are. And in that acceptance is forgiveness, humbleness, insight, wisdom and knowledge. Through these qualities, you can attract many blessings. Life is what you believe it to be and what you create in the moment.

I offer you now another story about a five-year-old girl who lived with her mother. The young girl was told that her father had passed away when she was born and the mother worked long and hard to clothe and feed her daughter. Often, when the mother went to the river to wash the clothes, she would take the young girl with her. At the river, the young insightful girl was quiet and played by herself for long periods of time.

One day, a woman stranger approached the mother and asked her if she desired the riches of the world?

The mother in her folly simply said, "Who would not?," and went on with her cleaning.

The stranger then replied, "If you so desire, I can make you rich."

At this point the young girl's mother stopped her cleaning and looked up at the stranger, aware that something was unusual. "What do you ask of me in return?" she asked knowing full well that any riches would require a price.

The stranger said, "I will take your daughter for five years and when I return her, both of you shall be rich."

The mother knew that what this woman suggested was likely nonsense, but nevertheless the mother pondered the thought of having riches over losing time with her daughter. But finally after a great deal of thought the mother turned to the stranger and said, "I have all that I need."

"You are wise," said the stranger.

"No" said the mother. "I am a fool because if I was truly wise, I would not have even considered what you had asked of me."

The stranger just smiled, turned away and knew that the fool was the wisest of all who lived because only the fool will allow himself to dream and only the fool will allow himself to love. And it is the fool who learns in life that happiness is created from pain, if one is only willing to go through it in order to rise above it. The mother could see that there was life beyond poverty but could not imagine a life without the one she loved. So you see, my message is this: if there are roads to take in life, take them, if there are dreams you have, dream them, if there are lands to conquer, travel them. But if in your dreams and travels, you do not discover what is important to you, you will not understand what is valuable. And if you do not understand that you are a part of everything you do, then to dream and to travel is pointless. To expect others to instinctively understand your dreams is to believe you are alone in a world with no support or love. But to share your desires and goals with others is to understand there is always a voice that is listening, and you will hear that voice if you listen closely to what you say, do and what you become.

I will relay one more story about a young eighteen-year-old man who came to me once during my travels. Knowing well his many difficulties, I forgave him for what he believed were his sins and helped him start a new life. On many occasions, we spoke at length and he told me once about his love for another person at the age of thirteen. This love for another remained undying and although he tried to run from it, it pursued him wherever he went. He had since become married in order to find himself and his responsibilities as well as to please his parents, family and friends.

"But to what penance must I do," he asked, "in order for this pain of love to be released so that I can get on with my life and my purpose?"

I looked into the young man's eyes and said, "Your purpose is what you are trying to escape from."

He replied, "Brother, it is not permissible to love one of my own."

I waited for some time before I responded and then said, "Each day the birds sing in the trees, the winds blow through the valley and the mountains stand high and proud overlooking the world. But do the mountains say, 'I cannot see?,' does the wind say, 'I cannot breathe?,' do the birds say, 'I cannot sing?' And so, should you say to me that you cannot love?

"But I shall be banished and turned away from my home to the streets if I love another of my own kind."

"And so the streets shall become your home," I said.

"Why am I so challenged in this life" he replied, "for I am strong and can do much, but this love for another man keeps me weak?"

"To love another person is not wrong, unjust, criminal or against the beliefs of God. In this moment you believe that you are vulnerable because you feel love and are trying to deny that which is most natural to you. Many try to deny that which is natural to them and live in trees like birds that do not sing. And so, you live in a world with no music, no breath, no sight and no life."

"But what of those who oppose me and wish to see me dead?," he asked.

"Allow yourself to die singing, than to live life dead."

SESSION 27

It is interesting to see how the world and its people have become so divided. Where is this loss of faith in one another, where has the trust gone and where is the compassion and zest for life? Why is it that so many people are tired and discreetly desire to no longer exist? Is it that so many souls have gone through too many challenges or is it that as a collective source we have lost our understanding of what we are here to accomplish?

If you look at all of the world's religions whether it involves praying to God or no God at all, whether there is a belief in myself, Jesus Christ, or some other deity, there is one common element which is simply a belief in something. However, what hinders you in your progress ironically are your beliefs just as they also help you to grow, for to believe in an all-powerful God, does not mean that you believe He will heal you. With time and understanding you can unlock the wealth of information which will help you unleash the power within yourself to heal, to know and to understand. You will see that a divine power, or whatever you wish to call it, lies within you and it is both your slave and your master. How you use it, harness it and release it, and whether you use it to heal, is up to you in each of your lifetimes.

If you do not release it, it does not make you a good or bad person. You will simply live where you are, being where you are, doing what you do. When you have found your God, you will understand the God that I found. When you speak to your God, you will know the God that I spoke to. When you feel at peace with yourself, you will know the peace that I felt. And when you pass into spirit, you will discover all of the glory and beauty that exists in your physical world as well as in the spiritual realm. It is then that your purpose for existing will come to your conscious thoughts and you will know why you are here and why you exist. But whether you are consciously aware of your purpose or not, you can still forge ahead and look for a reason and purpose in all that you do, whether you believe it exists or not. Some think that the search for God and myself is the ultimate experience, but in offering us your praise, you may block your own need to be loved and your own requirements for inner peace. If you believe in yourself and the love and the God that exists within you, there would be no need for praise because you could accept the idea that everything is a part of who you are which in itself needs no explanation or praise. I am not saying that it is not good to pray or to meditate but when you pray, internalize your prayers and pray from your heart and soul. The God you need to reach is the God that exists within you, and that God within you is connected to everything outside of you.

To find a place within yourself is the point you arrive at after a long journey of realizing your resolutions to a problem. You believe that in death you will discover many answers but you know the answers now, you just believe you do not. So by understanding yourself, you will have a clearer idea about what exists beyond you and by trusting yourself you will have a sense that others can also be trusted. With time, as you learn to lay down your armour and drop your swords and spears, you will see that it was only fear that kept you guarded and only fear that kept you apart from your fellow peers. Fear keeps you from embracing yourself and the love that you have within. To arm yourself with words and thoughts of being attacked is to fear and believe that you are unloved and unprotected.

I walked to my death believing in God, but I also held fear, not about whether God existed, but about the ensuing pain that would result. Therefore, I faltered in my belief in a God that was loving, caring, knowing and seeing. If I did not falter, however, would I not have been human? The spirit, the God and the soul within you understands the obstacles of your physical world and you will have many falters. Thus, the test is to listen, to believe, to know and to trust. The answer to your life is to have peace, but to achieve peace, you must know pain, and to know pain is to lose love or never know that you have had it.

When your journey is complete and all who love or hate you gather around for one last time will you look at them and judge them for their human qualities, or see your own follies and disbeliefs about humanity? Will you recognize that you have lived in a world of fool's gold, or pretend that all you believe is how others see it? When death stands at your side what is important and what will your thoughts turn to. Your purpose? Who has loved you? Who you have loved or what you could have done better? Would you turn to death and embrace it as you would embrace love for if death is disguised as love in your living state, is love disguised as death?..When you choose to embrace love, are you embracing pain?..Do you know love's smile or is it an illusion that mocks you at every turn?..Do you live for years believing in love's grace when love is not there to be felt? Does your God require that you live in isolation without love, or must you find the love that exists within yourself? Must you travel through the darkness and stillness of the night in order to see the depths of solitude, pain and loneliness before awakening to the love that exists within? If you do not make the journey into the desert, will you spend your life afflicted with thoughts of what could have been? Will you find the lips that whisper the words, "I love you?"

Your heart rings hollow because you do not know what love is. So you question, again and again, which devils haunt your thoughts and movements. If you know your journey is short, will you embrace the little time you have and laugh to yourself or cry with another? Will your children smile upon you for taking up the challenge to overcome the pain, or will they repeat the same patterns that you have repeated from your parents?

These questions may appear confusing and you may be unsure of what I speak, but it is not love that I doubt. What I doubt is what you do not trust. So each individual must learn to trust with his or her heart, soul and mind. The gifts of love and compassion are rarely accepted and what is considered as logical is often a defense for ignorance. I leave you with this question: When you have captured your heart and when you have harnessed the power of your soul and relinquished the control of your mind, what will you do with your senses?

SESSION 28

Alaix, Alaix, Alaix - This word has great significance in your world, your culture and your lifestyle alongside so many other things that are taken for granted. In a time long before I lived as Jesus Christ, words were utilized to open the ethers. Certain words had the power to initiate a feeling of purity or evil as you call it now; one feeling would create abundance and another devastation. Throughout history, however, it was the Masters who carried these words and cherished and guarded them with great importance. Words were eventually misused and brought about great chaos and destruction, and were lost to the evolution of humankind. During those periods, somewhere in the vicinity of 20,000 BC, using words, images of monsters and demons could be conjured up at will and many practiced this art to enhance their power. And so, sorcery was looked upon as a powerful, albeit archaic, tool. Still today, the average individual fears it and the seemingly powerful admire it since the energy of these words will always exist.

Not everyone is born with a beautiful voice, a beautiful face or a warm personality. Some are born with their gifts well hidden and only use the talents they are aware of to help them complete simple tasks. Both Einstein and Van Gogh are great historical figures whose gifts were initially disguised but were eventually hailed as strong examples of success. Yet there are others such as Caesar, Napoleon and Hitler who were thought to be incredibly gifted in the moment but were eventually despised because of the abuse of their gifts. So I ask, to what means does one measure quality and quantity and how can you be certain that the stranger you come to speak with may not be the most radiant of souls? It is conceivable that in the past you yourself had great knowledge in the area of witchcraft and magic, but the issue is whether one's gifts are used for positive or negative objectives.

Around the year 2010, as I mentioned in an earlier session, two ancient documents containing powerful words will be discovered once again. Two individuals will make this discovery and will work hard to understand them. In time others will follow. What I am pointing out here is that history is repeating and the opportunity to grow and learn, to see, hear and know again has fallen on everyone's doorstep. You may or may not be aware that religion is one of the most, if not the world's most powerful institution. If you tried to understand how it has impacted your knowledge and success, you would need to look far beyond my years as Jesus Christ. At one time, in many cultures, there was one individual who led the masses and was accepted as a God of great strength and insight. It was believed that this person's powerful gifts were passed along through the generations and it is within this idea that royalty was created. Those seemingly noble individuals who ruled the lands were given the role of power and understood the abilities of the universe and what it had to offer. Not just through knowledge but through wisdom did these elite people use their abilities. However, while one individual may be wiser for his status, he can easily fall prey to greed, pride and jealousy.

You may believe that witchery and evil no longer exist but in reality they do. At the time I lived, when seeking advice, you questioned not one but all of the elders and their collective power. I was a threat because the elders knew I did not fear them for to me power and status had little meaning and I knew they used it only in the pursuit of greater material wealth and power. Had they used their gifts for the benefit of the whole they may have embraced me warmly, but they did not. The elders feared that I would reveal them for who they were, yet I had no desire to free them from their prisons. I had come forth only to give my word to those who desired to listen. Those who feared me, only saw in themselves their own fear of living and dying, and what they expected from me as their punishment was a result of what they had done to others. The little happiness that they did acquire did not come from those who were around them but from those they took from.

When you learn to meditate and turn your energy inward, words will come like keys to open the doors of your understanding, therefore allow yourself to hear them. Latin was commonly used during the 12th and 13th centuries and it was considered the language of those who were noble, honest and Christian. In Latin there were words that carried a certain energy to restore health, vitality, insight and wisdom to those who used them, but as many faltered along the way and lost their vision, so did the churches. Latin is considered to be a very old language and there are so many other ancient languages that have also been used in a similar fashion throughout history.

The English language will never disappear, but then you cannot see the future nor fully understand your past. There are no physical demons as you have been taught, but energies that are feared because they are unseen. These energies cannot harm you unless you allow them to, much the same way you can allow a relationship to hurt you when you are in love. To begin a relationship with someone is to accept the problems and difficulties that may arise from that relationship. Should you decline, there is probably an awareness that something does not feel right. This is the principle that many religions and historical figures use to mobilize the masses.

If you looked into the future, you would see the many changes unraveling, some quickly and others not. So many individuals are quick to discredit anything of value, yet are unable to make a decision for themselves. You search for answers through avenues that at one time you would not have even considered. However, if you were truly responsible for your emotions, thoughts and understood your actions, would you really need another individual to show you the way?

You are falling ill with poor health and your desire to have someone save you is growing stronger. But how did your sickness originate in the first place? What will you learn from it and how will it show you the way out? If you are diseased, is it possible to let go of it? Is it possible to believe that it can be released? What fears do you need to overcome? If you think that the world revolved around you, what would happen if you were removed from it? Would the world continue to evolve from the other billions of people who live here?

When you come to a self-centred and powerful place of thought, heart, soul and physical well-being, it is at this point where you will begin to find what you are looking for in life.

SESSION 29

I often spoke to the multitudes about future events. In your words, you would call them predictions but to me the very discussion of these events was a part of evolution, something that each soul will eventually understand over time. To help you understand the time when I lived, I used to tell a story about a young child who travelled from lifetime to lifetime, changing identity and growing with each journey. I explained that the child would go through a metamorphosis called "death" and during death, much like a caterpillar evolving to a butterfly, its soul would mature and take on a new identity.

By changing its identity, the child was able to learn many different things and see life through varying shades of colour. If you look around you, you will understand that the period of time in which you now live shall return again with new developments, but it will be a building upon the past growing in learning and insight. The degree to which the child would develop from each passing life varied with its accumulation of lifetimes. Now I turn this story onto you. You have passed through many different lifetimes and although the child within your soul is young, your feet are weary and your journey long. You are tired of repeating the same mistakes, as well as of the pain and confusion that comes with each new identity. In this life, you want to break free from the shackles that bind you and discover the essence, purpose and totality of all consciousness. This is the reason why you exist and why you must travel through each lifetime.

Although it is a demanding challenge to comprehend the total consciousness of all that is, you can. Your understanding of who and what you are is limited by your fear and by the illusions you perpetuate around you, including the illusion concerning your purpose. Nevertheless, you desire and want to know more, to go beyond the obstacles and the physical world that teaches you to sense things you cannot quite touch. You want to know your purpose to understand what you live for and it is a painful destiny to live when you do not believe.

Surrounded by so many people with varying gifts, it is hard to know where you fit in. It is also incomprehensible to believe that from all of your lifetimes that this one can last for a brief moment before you perish. If you picture the world with all of its inhabitants and the numerous lifetimes and existences that each of us have had, somewhat like one huge tear falling from a giant's eye, you may gain a sense of how many other worlds, purposes and existences lie beyond this one tear. Within this tear is the essence of the giant's heart whose purpose we explain through feeling and emotion, but it is also true that this giant is a part of another world, of another tear that you cannot possibly comprehend. A part of who I am is a part of what you wish to discover about yourself through each of your lifetimes, and as you travel through every door and every existence, you gather more information to know that there is so much beyond what you perceive. Although you are a small part of what exists around you, you are an equal part, no less and no more than any animal, plant or living thing. All that is around you lives and breathes a certain type of energy. To believe that you are superior is folly but this belief is also a part of your nature in being human just as the lion is perceived to be superior in its own domain, and Mother Nature superior in Hers.

It is necessary to see beyond your walls in order to achieve balance, harmony and contentment which will help you to understand your limitations and the purpose for your existence. To go beyond your walls and your limitations is to understand existence in its purest form. If I was to remove you from your obstacles and beliefs in this moment, would you still have purpose or would you develop even stronger capabilities beyond all others? Would you see farther, hear deeper and recognize the limitless potential within each human? Would you challenge yourself to create a world without despair, limitations or beliefs? In your purest form, you would understand that death is inevitable and that your only purpose is to live in harmony with one another to create a better world.

If you looked at each country and imagined that one nation which borders another could fight its neighbour the way they do, you would see the pain each country needlessly inflicts upon the other. To move beyond war you must first recognize that the enemy resides at home, not abroad, and to kill your brother and sister is to kill yourself. In answer to the question of whether war has a purpose, my answer is yes. War exists to show us the defeat we experience at our own hands because to battle for what is unimportant is to believe that we are still caged and will never break through the walls of ignorance. It is possible that the fatigue you carry in your feet from all the travels of your lifetimes shows that it is time to change and time to go beyond the old and embrace the new. But the 'new' will include the lost and forgotten laws and insights that have already passed through history. They will resurface once again and when they do, embrace the change, adopt the new and live for one another. In doing so, you will create opportunities for yourself and others, and develop a purpose beyond any described before in history.

SESSION 30

In the final phase of your life on earth, there is a completion that takes place on a subconscious level. Consciously you are partially aware but do not fully recognize the implications of what is happening around you. To understand my point further, someone young who is about to travel to the other side of the veil, will instinctively draw close to family to express emotional desires, feeling and thoughts. This individual will complete small tasks that are significant to him or her and finish off old relationships that have been left incomplete.

In life, you always have the opportunity to complete things that are important to you, on an emotional, physical, mental and spiritual level. It is the soul's ultimate goal to achieve harmony but outwardly it is difficult for you as a person to conquer constant emotional and physical conflicts that occur with passing time. If you are consciously aware and desire completion, then your soul can force situations and opportunities for completion to happen. For example, if you have an argument with a friend but wish to resolve the conflict even after a number of years, your soul and the universe will force the opportunity to arise, whether in a dream or physical waking state, to harmonize this situation.

I mention this to assist you in being more aware of the situations you have left uncompleted. When a certain energy, such as an argument, remains unresolved from other lifetimes, you will be forced back to complete it. This is why when you meet someone even for a short period of time, you may feel an incredibly strong connection to them and may walk away feeling as if something was finished. It may be a simple "hello" to a stranger, or a chance meeting that will provide you a conclusion.

Other situations may all be resolved in a similar fashion. Often times in family situations all siblings, parents, husbands, wives or children are each souls you have been closely connected to in numerous other lifetimes. There are other occasions when you experience a deep connection with someone but have had no other lives together, and this type of connection provides an opportunity to manifest your purpose. You could easily say that there is a reason for every situation which transpires in your life, but to take it to such extremes can make you irrational and obsessed. It is far better to let your natural senses harmonize with the soul and operate automatically on where you need to go and what you need to do. You are programmed from a soul level but that programming involves free choice, though the choice to do what you are doing was made at the start of time. In other words, you have set into motion a sequence of events that will give you the experience and insight you desire, and although you are following through on your perceived destiny, destiny itself is a choice that was created by you, for you, a long time ago. And still, within your soul, is the choice to change events and circumstances at any time, however rare, simply because you, as a soul, live in the physical world to gain certain experiences and must follow through on what you choose.

The reason for existing and understanding more about yourself is to create greater harmony and insight for your soul because what you program and what you manifest are not always the same. When your soul first originated, it may have had an idea of how it would evolve through its many different lifetimes, but as you physically manifested and developed, your soul may have discovered further obstacles and assets along the way that it did not expect. So the soul becomes wiser through its experiences and as it gains strength, it gains greater choice.

To see beyond your physical world is to see beyond death and beyond words because the language beyond words is one spoken in death. To know that you know who you are and why you are here but believe you have no purpose is and can be a totally and completely fulfilling experience. You may feel satisfied to know you are nothingness, empty energy in a void, expressionless with no expression. When you can know nothingness, you also can understand death's experience and the meaning beyond it. You can realize that death has no hold on your soul, but only with your physical heart rooted strongly within your physical domain. To reach beyond what you physically know is to create a far greater and wider path for yourself to follow.

Though I knew well my pathway as Jesus Christ, it did not make my experiences easier when I lived because my physical reality challenged my soul in ways I cannot explain. You can know at a soul level that you are wise but also that you will die at a young age and on a physical, mental and emotional level, you may feel cheated and robbed of life. While your soul is wise and provides much understanding and knowledge, you are still bounded by the physical world that re-emphasizes the idea that you believe you are incapable of certain things. Your physical reality constantly expects you to be greedy, upset, emotional, confused, discouraged and unloved. These emotions keep you from reaching beyond what is real; they keep you from knowing what you are about and the richness of what lies within. To look at anyone in your life, to think beyond their physical bodies and to tune into the light of their soul, you would feel blessed at your ability; you would feel empowered. You would understand the true essence of love, of brotherhood and sisterhood, of camaraderie and love beyond words and expectations. But few if any know how to think beyond this physical world and how to tune into someone else's light and if you do not even know what your own light holds, how can you possibly know another's? There are times when you have glimpses of someone's light and energy and you are uncertain about what you see and if your senses deceive you. You believe you have seen something beautiful but you will question it until you destroy it with your doubts.

Relationships are also ruined through improper thoughts and doubts. You look and see beauty but when you speak, you destroy. You do not take the opportunity to capture the initial beauty or light that radiated for only a split second before it disappeared. As you delve into another person's energy and light, you begin to discover their issues and problems, and quickly assume that they are not worthy of your time. However, if they are not worthy, are you also not worthy? Perhaps the glimpse of light and beauty you originally saw was your own beauty reflected back through their eyes, but afterwards your shame, disgust and the fears within yourself began to surface and were reflected back to you again.

To capture what is truly valuable, you must look beyond one's eyes and the deception of the mirror reflected back to you. You must look deep within your soul at what you have truly harnessed within. Ask not what the person can give to you, ask only to recognize the light that is a part of what resides within you. All lights in the world shed brightness, some stronger then others, but if you removed your physical body and travelled with it, you would discover that everyone shares the same light. You would discover a world radiant and rich in love, harmony and spiritual growth for at the core of all beings is a magnificent pearl of light, too beautiful to express in words. You constantly try to unlock the secret code that will get you inside of your soul, and enable you to love yourself and the beauty that you possess. If you could decipher that code and get through, even for a brief moment, what would you see? What will you discover that you possess? What will you come to know? Will you reach the end of your journey? Will you know without a doubt that you are a part of all that exists? As you gaze at your own beautiful pearl, will you want to reach out to others and have them join you to create a brilliant circle of light? What do you want to capture if for one split second you could be in your purest form and exquisitely content at the core of your being?

So I ask, in your purpose of what you strive for, what do you desire to have in life? Will your material rewards bring you that one moment of ultimate fulfillment? Surely, as the waves pour forth from the ocean into the glass of life and then are released upon the shore, they will become still and quiet in reaching their destination. But then, after a moment of stillness, other waves will follow, each finding their purpose, though they do not know where they began nor where they ended. As you drink the water from the glass of life, do you encompass the waves that have lapped up onto the shore?

In your final quest to understand all that is around you, is it difficult to see that within that pearl of life, your wave from the ocean will eventually find the shore, and the peace and beauty of its resting place? Your quest and destiny are one just as all people together are one. As you find completion in your soul, you will also understand what I have said, what I have revealed and the essence and value of the pearl and the beauty that encompass everything that exists. Humanity has a destiny to discover the pearl that lies within the ocean and to recognize its beauty that is beyond expression.

SESSION 31 (A)

You may sense throughout this last session a variation in vibrations and energy. There will be a number of souls that will come together through me today, most prominently Mother Cabrini along with other historically well known souls who will appear in combination with my self. However, it will not appear so obvious which soul has come through. Today we close and so the three of you[6] are here with me to perform the closure of this session.

In completing this book, to all three of you I say, remember always that you walk with me and I walk with you. There are no endings to any books. The story continues as does life, and I shall continue as each of you shall continue long after this life.

To this soul whom I speak through, Dale Landry, I admire his grace and talent and his ability to push forward amidst adversity and constant upheaval. Life often expects much from one who can give little but has given so much. The key has been turned and the door is now open. Together we shall make great strides.

My name Jesus Christ carries insight and many shall learn and see through this book. As each of you see success in the coming years, you will realize the wonderful opportunity you created to sit and listen to me speak and I do believe it unusual that it was only the three of you who chose to be here. It is ironic because when I lived as Christ there were only a few who truly listened and only a few who came. It was only after my departure that people saw and heard what I had to say. Yet as I sit here, I do not believe that the three of you fully hear my words since what you do is out of ritual and the fear that perhaps something good may pass you by. You must question yourself wether you really see, really hear, or really know? Or is it perhaps an illusion created by this soul that I speak through that covers my tracks so well? Perhaps I can be so easily overlooked since I am speaking through

---

6 The three individuals to whom Jesus Christ is referring is Rosaria Cioffi, Charles Ludlow and Christine Zeldin. Each sat in on all of the sessions to develop this book, "The Christ Spirit".

someone so average, so unassuming, so incapable of anything too spectacular. Or, perhaps like yourselves and the millions of other people like you, you will believe that you can be easily overlooked. Therefore, it is important to give yourselves the acknowledgement that you would give others whom you would see in this moment as important.

SESSION 31(B)

There was a time when I journeyed far from my home to seek the wisdom of a great guru. I travelled to an unknown land of great valleys, hills and mountains. The soul I sought lived high on the mountainside and had four keepers to assist in this guru's soul purpose. When I reached this guru, the keepers knew well that I was coming and embraced me and welcomed me as if I was one of their own.

For four days and nights I worked amongst them, spoke with them, learned of their experiences and insight, and felt renewed in my life purpose. But I wondered why the soul I had come to speak to had not appeared. Listening to my heart, however, I knew I had to wait patiently for my opportunity. On the fifth day as I was preparing to leave, one of the keepers came to me and said that the guru was ready to speak.

I went with the keeper to a small room where a beautiful young woman sat close to a stone fireplace. The keeper asked me to sit next to her and to take her hand. At first I was confused for I had expected this guru to be a man and much older than she was. But knowing well how I had fooled myself many times before, I gladly took my place and held her hand in mine.

I sat with her for what seemed to be an eternity, although I am sure it was just a few short moments. The silence grew thick and although words were spoken, nothing was said. Finally, without expression, she spoke aloud.

"You do not see that I am blind?"

I waited a moment to reply, "No, I was not aware."

"Could you not sense it?" the guru asked.

Again I took a moment to think and replied honesty, "No, I did not sense it."

She then explained that even without her sight, she saw clearly who I was. "You have come seeking wisdom and insight from someone who is old and experienced, but you find someone that is young and blind. Does your sight fool you?" she continued.

"Yes, it does."

"And now that you have had time to sit with me, what does your sight and ignorance tell you now?"

"It tells me little, except that you have travelled far and know many things I do not."

"And if I was old and experienced, would I have travelled less but just as far?"

"I do not understand," I said to her.

"Your eyes blind you from insight and yet without sight I have travelled far and experienced much in a very short period of time. So you are more challenged with sight because you are less able to see. I am less challenged because without sight I have a stronger visual ability. You have come looking for wisdom and my reply to you is to lose your sight. For when you are unable to see, you will not judge, and when you can no longer judge you will know love and light and you will not try to capture it. Love and life are intangible; you cannot see them. So with sight, you are blind."

At this point she explained that it was time for me to leave but I did not want to.

"Why do you hesitate?" she asked.

"I believe that I have come home and I do not wish to go."

"Can you not take home with you?" she asked.

Again I was lost. "To capture these few moments that I have with you seems incomprehensible to me and so to take it with me, I do not know of what you speak."

She continued, "What you do not see is that as you leave, you take my heart with you and I too must suffer the pain of your loss. But I must also live for that moment when I shall be home again. You are not the only one pained in life who suffers in isolation and loneliness, but still your voice within shatters all, yet, speaks loudly to guide us.

Though I must let you go to speak of the words we have spoken, I also have pain in my heart for I understand love, its grasp and also its strength."

In my foolishness I asked whether we would meet again in this life and regretted asking the question, since it was the weakness of my heart that betrayed me.

"No we will not," she replied.

As I stood to leave and made my way to the door, my feet felt heavy and laden. After only a few steps, I turned back to look at her and saw that she was not there and a voice out of nowhere said to me, "What do you see?"

"I see nothing."

And she replied, "Now you are blind and your journey complete for in the future when you meet those of true heart, you will not see them, nor will you be able to touch them."

"I know now why I have come," I said.

"And why is that?" she asked.

"I came here to know that I have a friend."

"You have made a very long journey for a friend," she said.

"When one looks and sees nothing and travels long distances to see something that is not there, one understands his or her journey."

"I shall leave you with this," she said. "My voice, though it calls from afar, shall bridge the distance of our two souls and when your heart speaks and your sight disappears, know that you have found me once again."

As I left, I saw no one but heard voices speaking and remembered well the woman's gift. In my life, I had always used words to see but never saw beyond them. When I returned home, my mother Mary greeted me and, upon hearing my voice, asked what I had learned on my journey.

Gazing into my mother's eyes, she felt the heaviness of my heart and knew well what I spoke of and what I had learned. While my mother and I spoke often in thought, never before had she seen or felt as I did because I had never been capable of feeling as a man. And in her thoughts, she understood that I had found the pain of manhood with its strength of emotion.

"What shall your message be now to those whom you speak to in your travels?" she asked in her eyes.

"I shall tell them all to be blind and to have heart."

"But will they understand?" she asked.

"No," I said, "but I do not fully understand it either."

That night when I turned in to sleep, the Archangel Michael appeared once again at the foot of my bed and sat quietly to hear my words.

"You are no longer wise," he said. "What has happened?"

"I am able to feel but I have no words."

"Does that make you blind?" he asked.

"Yes," I answered.

"What do you fear in your blindness?" he asked.

"That I no longer have answers."

"Do you need answers when you feel?" he asked.

"I do not know," I replied.

To that response he was gone and I was left with my unknowing.

As I unraveled thought after thought in my mind as one would unravel a scroll, I saw a new door opening and another one closing. With that I understood my whole purpose as Jesus Christ. It was not to be wise or experienced, but to feel the experience and wisdom of blindness because on earth, all are blind. And it is through the blind heart that one speaks often to the soul and the soul, its only friend, carries with it the experience of life's journey through to the end.

To you I bless, and may your feet be heavy and your sight be blind, in order that you may see more clearly your purpose and the love that surrounds you.

TO CONTACT THE AUTHOR

Dear Reader, Seminar Coordinator or Meeting Planner:

Both the publisher and author want to know how you enjoyed *"The Christ Spirit"*...Please note that not every response can be answered. To provide comments, write to the address shown below.

To help ensure a reply, please enclose a self-addressed, stamped envelope or international postal reply coupon.

Dale Landry has been working and developing psychically as a trance channeller since 1983. He has been interviewed on Canada's *The Dini Petty Show*, Toronto's *640 AM*, national talk show *Jane Hawtin* as well as numerous other radio and television programs. Mr. Landry is available for events, seminars and workshops. For more information, please write, phone or fax:

The Access Publishers Network Inc.
6893 Sullivan Rd.
Brawn, Michigan
U.S.A. 49637

Phone: 1-800-345-0096

Fax: 1800-950-9793

The Christ Spirit
ISBN 0-9684678-1-4

OR
Hushion House Publishing Limited
36 Northline Road
Toronto, Ontario
Canada M4B 3E2

Phone: 1-800-387-0141 **Ontario/Quebec**

           1-800-387-0172 **All other provinces**

Fax: (416) 285-1777